WHERE TO FROM HERE?

About the Authors

Dr. Philip Curry is a social psychologist based at the School of Social Work and Social Policy, Trinity College Dublin. He currently teaches research methods for the Masters in Applied Social Research programme and conducts research on issues related to children and migration.

Professor Robbie Gilligan is Head of the School of Social Work and Social Policy, and Associate Director of the Children's Research Centre, at Trinity College Dublin. He is currently President of Childwatch International.

Lindsey Garratt is a graduate of University College Dublin (Sociology and English) and is currently undertaking a PhD based in the Children's Research Centre, Trinity College Dublin.

Jennifer Scholtz is a graduate of University College Dublin (Sociology and Social Policy) and is currently undertaking a PhD based in the Children's Research Centre, Trinity College Dublin.

WHERE TO FROM HERE?

Inter-ethnic Relations among Children in Ireland

Philip Curry
Robbie Gilligan
Lindsey Garratt
Jennifer Scholtz

*Trinity Immigration Initiative
Children, Youth and Community Relations Project*

The Liffey Press

Published by
The Liffey Press
Ashbrook House, 10 Main Street
Raheny, Dublin 5, Ireland
www.theliffeypress.com

© 2011 Children's Research Centre, Trinity College Dublin

A catalogue record of this book is
available from the British Library.

ISBN 978-1-905785-98-8

All rights reserved. No part of this publication may be reproduced or transmitted in any form or by any means, including photocopying and recording, without written permission of the publisher. Such written permission must also be obtained before any part of this publication is stored in a retrieval system of any nature. Requests for permission should be directed to The Liffey Press, Ashbrook House, 10 Main Street, Raheny, Dublin 5, Ireland.

Printed in the United Kingdom by MPG Biddles.

'An only life can take so long to climb
Clear of its wrong beginnings, and may never ...'
– *Philip Larkin*

Contents

Acknowledgements ix

Preface xi

1. Migrant Children and Inter-ethnic Relations among Irish Primary School Children: A Research Review 1

2. A Case Study in North Inner-City Dublin[1] 21

3. Entering the Social World of Children 31

4. Migrant and Local Children: Different Languages, Values and Experiences 48

5. Social Interaction 1: Learning Together 87

6. Social Interaction 2: Distance and Separateness 108

7. Social Interaction 3: Prejudice, Bullying and Their Consequences 123

8. Where To from Here? Policy Challenges 163

9. Where To from Here? Possible Futures for Inter-ethnic Relations in Ireland 184

Appendix: The Children, Youth and Community Relations Research Programme 193

References 197

---

[1] This chapter was authored by Philip Curry, Robbie Gilligan and Derek Murphy.

Acknowledgements

First and foremost, we wish to thank all the children that took part in this project and their parents who allowed them to do so.

We sincerely thank the schools in Dublin's north inner-city that lent us enormous support in conducting this research. We would like to thank all the school principals, teachers and school staff who took part and otherwise facilitated this project.

We wish to thank The Children's Research Centre at Trinity College for hosting the project and the generous support of Professor Sheila Greene, Kathleen Lyons and Siobhan O'Brien.

In conducting this research, we had excellent support from three wonderful research assistants: Derek Murphy, Elizabeth O'Rourke and Kate Babineau.

We would also like to thank Dr. Muireann Ní Raghallaigh of UCD for her advice and participation in the project.

This book has benefited greatly from the painstaking and intelligent reading of Gerry Danaher and Deirdre Kirwan.

Finally, we would like to thank each of the following for their support: the Trinity Immigration Initiative and all of its members, Rebecca Alexis, David Connolly, Stephen Falvey, Gerry Folan, Seanie Lambe, Leslie McCarthy, Fergus McCabe, Molly O'Duffy, Dr. Margaret Rogers and Amel Yacef.

Preface

This book grows out of a project that examined social interaction between children of different cultural and ethnic groups attending Dublin north inner-city primary schools. The study set out to obtain a balanced account of life in multi-cultural schools and communities from the perspective of children. We believe that studying these issues among this age group is vital as this 'first generation' of multi-cultural Ireland will do much to determine the future tenor of inter-ethnic relations in this country. At the time of writing, it appears that things are still fluid and that attitudes could 'settle' in a number of different ways.

Studying inter-ethnic relations among children between the ages of 5 and 12 is important because:

- Multi-cultural attitudes, experiences and interaction among these children will form a very strong foundation for the future, both for themselves and for the communities in which they grow up.

- There is great potential for all of these children to learn and benefit from correctly managed responses to diversity.

- Children in multi-cultural schools have opportunities to interact with people from other cultures that their parents will often miss. As such, they are in the forefront of integration. There is in fact some evidence to suggest that where children have positive inter-cultural experiences, this can help positively influence the attitudes of their parents.

- Children at this age are open to positive influences and spend a lot of time in structured environments which are ideal settings in which to foster positive attitudes. Dealing with problematic inter-group behaviour is more difficult later on, both in terms of accessing and influencing it.
- Migrant children will often benefit from the experience of migration and be more mature and culturally competent as a result. However, migration also brings challenges, and proper supports can help to ensure migrant children get the most out of their education experience and their interaction with peers.
- Because of language difficulties, social isolation and visible difference, some children who have migrated may be more vulnerable to serious social isolation and bullying and may face particular difficulties accessing support.

The title of this book, *Where To from Here?*, can be interpreted in a number of ways. The first, most immediate, sense is what the future holds for the children who took part in this study in terms of inter-ethnic relations. Beyond the immediate context of the study, we can also ask how this wider generation of children, especially those who are faced with the day-to-day realities of multi-culturalism, will relate to one another across ethnic and cultural difference as they move forward into adulthood. These are of course challenging questions to answer. The future is difficult to predict and contexts can differ substantially. However, we believe that this in-depth study of interaction between children hints at some of the main contours of the future inter-cultural landscape in our society. It is very likely that negative attitudes and outlooks which are unchallenged by the intense and open contact that occurs in primary school will also go unchallenged elsewhere. An associated question, which relates particularly (though not exclusively) to the migrant children in our study, is where they will go from here in terms of residency, academic attainment and employment. Predicting this is beyond the scope of this book. All we can do is flag the importance of such issues and document the abilities, hopes and aspirations that exist among this group of children. This research also reaches beyond the lives of children. We can ask what the attitudes and behaviours of these children reveal about the communities and wider social contexts in which they live now (and the directions in which these adults and communities are headed).

Another way of approaching the question *Where To from Here?* is to reflect upon the possible courses of action that might be taken to help improve more problematic strands of inter-ethnic interaction that are documented in the study. In a nutshell, the form that this book takes is to offer a detailed examination of social interaction between children attending Irish multi-cultural schools, and then to review policies that might serve to promote positive interactions across cultural difference. There are other ways we could have dealt with the results of this research. There is very rich material for analysis in terms of sociological, educational and psychological theory. We will adopt such approaches in other forums, but in this book our principal focus is on policy and policy development. What, if anything, should schools, communities and policy-makers do about the kinds of issues encountered in this research? It is a question for the reader as well as the authors. As we will see, there are few easy answers but we believe that it is a fundamentally important question that will not go away. We strongly suggest that now is the time to think about it.

Finally, a note on terminology, which in the field of migration and ethnicity can be very fraught. When does someone cease to be a migrant? Or a 'newcomer' in the language of hospitality used by the Department of Education and Skills? What sense do labels such as these have in relation to children born to migrant parents living in Ireland, children who may never have even left Irish soil? How should we refer to such children as a group? Can we refer to them collectively alongside more recent arrivals born of migrant parents? Most formulations which are workable in every day speech will be biased in one direction or another. We are left with the choice of such crude simplifications or elaborate, unwieldy codes suitable only for specialised audiences. We have to acknowledge that terminology in this context is laden and that the meaning of labels such as 'Irish' or 'migrant' may be an important field for contest. However, no satisfactory solutions offer themselves.

A great deal of this book is given over to the reporting of intensive qualitative research, and in this context we have used the terms used most consistently by all groups of our participants. We will use the term 'local' to refer to children born of two Irish national parents, generally of a long ancestry in Ireland. In speech, children and adults often refer to 'the local kids'. We may be tempted to regard the term as problematic as to qualify as 'local' would only require a person to live in the area. However, within the context, the word has a very specific meaning and captures some of the long settled and stable nature of the communities we studied. 'Migrant' will be used as a catch-all term to refer to children of migrant parents who themselves were either born in Ireland or arrived after birth. This terminology is crude and insufficient to mirror the complexities of the situations involved, but it will serve its function as long as we recognise the context in which it is being used and the limitations involved. Exceptions which do not fit into these broad categories will be noted in the text. Where we discuss the work of other authors, we strive to preserve their usages as much as possible.

This book consists of nine chapters. In the first, we review all the major research studies to date in Ireland which have a bearing on the issue of social interaction between migrant and local Irish children of primary school age. In the second, we discuss the case study logic of our research project and introduce our research site, north inner-city Dublin. We then discuss child-centred research methods and present evidence from our research which illustrates biases in adult perspectives on the social world of children. The main results of the project are then presented over four chapters covering differences in outlook between migrant and local children, positive social interaction, indifference and separateness and finally, prejudice and bullying. In the penultimate chapter we address the question 'where to from here?' in terms of policy challenges for the future. In the final chapter we summarise the principal findings and arguments in the book and consider the long-term outlook for inter-ethnic relations among children in Ireland.

Chapter1

Migrant Children and Inter-ethnic Relations among Irish Primary School Children: A Research Review

Interviewer: Would there have been people from any other countries when you first started?

Local girl 1: Not really, no.

Local girl 2: Just all Irish in my class when I started.

Two local girls, Fifth class

In this chapter we look at some basic statistical information on migrant children coming to Ireland, discuss the significance of these demographic changes for all children living here and reflect on the importance of inter-ethnic relationships among young children. The bulk of the chapter is then given over to reviewing existing Irish research on social relationships among children from different ethnic groups. Finally, we outline the approach and broad aims of the current study.

One of the features of the sudden growth in inward migration to Ireland which occurred from the late 1990s onwards was a sudden growth in the number of children living in Ireland who were not born in the State or were born to parents not born in the State. Between 1996 and 2002, the percentage of children under the age of 14 with nationalities other than Irish decreased from 4.6 per cent to 4.2 per cent. But by 2006, this figure had increased to 6.2 per cent. In absolute numbers, this represents an increase from 34,131 in 2002 to 52,500 in 2006. However, as we can see from Table 1, the apparent drop in the number of migrant children between 1996 and 2002 masks a demographic shift: a dramatic drop in the number of children of UK and US origin and an increase in the number of children of African and Asian origin. Between 2002 and 2006 we can see further large increases in the number of children of African and Asian origin, as well as a very large increase in the number of children of European nationality (reflecting the 2004 enlargement of the European Union). Looking at the same numbers from a different point of view shows that the period 1996 to 2006 saw a more than four-fold increase in the number of children of European nationalities (other than UK and US), a six-fold increase in Asian nationalities, and over nine-fold in African nationalities.

As well as the relatively sudden increase in immigration, a noticeable feature of the Irish immigration experience is its great diversity. Child migrants to Ireland have come from all over the globe. Table 2 gives us some sense of this. As we can see from the table, other than Irish, the largest national groups represented among children under 14 are United Kingdom (1.8 per cent), Nigeria (0.5 per cent), and USA (0.4 per cent). The numbers from any individual country tend to be small and a lot of countries are represented.

The picture is, in fact, much richer than Table 2 would suggest. Among all age groups, Census 2006 recorded 188 different nationalities (CSO, 2009). Many of these were made up of small numbers, but it does give us a strong sense of the huge diversity among migrants that have come to Ireland.

Table 1: Children 14 and under in Ireland by nationality group from 1996 to 2006[1]

	1996	2002	2006
Total Irish	816,115 (95.4%)	775,603 (94.1%)	797,281 (92.7%)
UK and US	31,332 (3.7%)	20,967 (2.5%)	19,186 (2.2%)
European nationality other than Ireland or UK	3,629 (0.4%)	4,811 (0.6%)	16,293 (1.9%)
Africa	840 (0.1%)	4,305 (0.5%)	7,647 (0.9%)
Asia	881 (0.1%)	1,888 (0.2%)	5,497 (0.6%)
Other nationalities	2,625 (0.3%)	1,688 (0.2%)	3,335 (0.4%)
Multi-nationality	Not available	472 (0.1%)	542 (0.1%)
No nationality	Not available	229 (0.0%)	397 (0.0%)
Not stated	Not available	13,916 (1.7%)	10,318 (1.2%)
TOTAL	855,422 (100%)	823,879 (100%)	860,496 (100%)

Source: CSO (1996, 2003, 2006)

---

[1] Note that the presence of high numbers in the *Not Stated* category means that the actual numbers in any given nationality group may be higher.

Table 2: Children 14 and under in Ireland by nationality

Nationality	N	%	Nationality	N	%
Total Irish	797,281	92.7%	Russia	653	0.1%
EU			Ukraine	316	0.0%
Austria	53	0.0%	Other Europe	1,256	0.1%
Belgium	69	0.0%	**Americas**		
Cyprus	5	0.0%	USA	3,535	0.4%
Czech Rep	356	0.0%	Brazil	446	0.1%
Denmark	61	0.0%	Canada	334	0.0%
Estonia	198	0.0%	Other America	297	0.0%
Finland	62	0.0%	**Africa**		
France	588	0.1%	Nigeria	4,151	0.5%
Germany	821	0.1%	South Africa	955	0.1%
Greece	32	0.0%	Other Africa	2,541	0.3%
Hungary	197	0.0%	**Asia**		
Italy	366	0.0%	China	412	0.0%
Latvia	1,238	0.1%	Philippines	1,572	0.2%
Lithuania	2,778	0.3%	India	1,162	0.1%
Luxembourg	4	0.0%	Pakistan	952	0.1%
Malta	17	0.0%	Malaysia	227	0.0%
Netherlands	418	0.0%	Other Asia	1,172	0.1%
Poland	4,790	0.6%			
Portugal	175	0.0%	Australia	568	0.1%
Slovakia	418	0.0%	New Zealand	147	0.0%
Slovenia	10	0.0%	Other Nationality	1,543	0.2%
Spain	277	0.0%	Multi-nationality	542	0.1%
Sweden	111	0.0%	No Nationality	397	0.0%
UK	15,651	1.8%	*Not stated*	10,318	1.2%
Rest of Europe			**TOTAL**	860,496	100%
Romania	1,024	0.1%			

Source: CSO (2008).

Although the total numbers of migrant children are relatively small, by Irish standards, this represents an enormous demographic shift. Of course, the full impact of these changes on communities and schools cannot be grasped until we understand that child migrants are not evenly distributed throughout the country. Taken as a whole, the migrant population is concentrated in Dublin city, Fingal, South Dublin, County Cork, Galway and in popular tourist destinations on the Western and Southern seaboards (CSO, 2009). Primary schools in particular seem to be differentially affected by migration. Smyth, Darmody, McGinnity and Byrne (2009) found that approximately 10 per cent of all primary school children are newcomers, and further estimated that:

- While 90 per cent of second-level schools have newcomer students, only 56 per cent of primary schools have.
- Almost half of the second level schools have between 2 per cent and 9 per cent newcomer students. Primary schools in general tend to have higher proportions or none at all.
- Almost one in ten primary schools has over 20 per cent newcomers.
- Primary schools are more likely to have more newcomer students if they are urban, disadvantaged and large.

We will return to the possible explanation of such patterns in Chapter 3. For now, we can simply note that many primary schools and the communities which they serve have experienced a profound demographic shift, bringing with it both challenges and opportunities. With the economic downturn, we may expect some further change in these patterns. However, data available to date clearly indicate that many migrants who came here in the 'boom' period are staying (CSO, 2009, 2010). Multi-culturalism would appear now to be a permanent feature of most childhoods in Ireland.

The main focus of the study reported in this book is on the social interactions between migrant children and their local counterparts. Although these phenomena are new to the Irish experience, there is a large body of international literature which tells us that inter-ethnic and inter-cultural relations are issues that should be taken seriously among even very young children. This literature is vast having developed over, at least, a 75-year period. In this section, we will draw attention to just two main points from this literature: firstly, the early age at which awareness of ethnicity emerges, and secondly, the broad context in which we should understand inter-ethnic relations.

Adults can seriously underestimate the significance that young children will attach to group signifiers such as race and nationality. Since the very earliest days of social research, there has been consistent evidence that children are 'aware of cues that adults designate as "racial"' (Katz, Sohn and Zalk, 1975). This had been found as early as the pioneering studies of Clark and Clark (1939, 1947) and since then a huge body of evidence has been gathered which demonstrates that ethnic awareness can emerge as early as three or four years of age (Aboud, 1988; Levy and Killen, 2008). In a more local context, Connelly, Smith and Kelly (2002), in their study entitled *Too Young to Notice?*, found that children in Northern Ireland began to show small but significant preferences for Catholic or Protestant symbols and public representatives by the age of three and that such preferences grew stronger by the age of five and six.

Awareness of ethnic difference and preferences for groups of which one is a member does not necessarily imply problematic behaviour such as prejudice and bullying. However, such behaviours can occur and can be understood as part of a continuum ranging from open and positive, to negative, hostile and derogatory. In some social research, there has been a tendency to isolate and focus on negative behaviours. However, today, many of the theoretical frameworks used to understand social interaction between different cultural groups emphasise that we should understand problematic inter-ethnic behaviour in a broader context, for example that of general inter-group relations (Tajfel, 1978) or the acculturation strategies and attitudes of both individuals and communities (Berry, 2001). For now, the key points are that a large amount of international evidence tells us that even very young children are aware of group and ethnic identities and that problematic or positive attitudes and beliefs about national and ethnic identity can develop very early.

An Overview of Research in the Irish Context

A number of studies have directly or indirectly looked at how experiences of social interaction in Irish primary schools have been affected by migration. Given that there are a limited number of such studies, and that they form an essential context for the present research, we will treat each in some detail, looking in each case at the methodology and key findings. We will focus mainly on the results concerning primary schools and social interaction. However, we will also include some findings concerning the academic performance, attitude to education and language competency among migrant pupils because, as we shall see later, these all have an important bearing on our understanding of migrant children's social interaction with local children. Throughout this book, we will attempt to synthesise these studies, both with each other and with our own findings.

The work of Dympna Devine and colleagues

The earliest, and most relevant, study for our purposes is a report, commissioned by the Department of Education and Science, entitled *Ethnicity and Schooling: A Study of Ethnic Diversity in Selected Irish Primary and Post-primary Schools* by Dympna Devine and Máirín Kenny (2002). This report is based on a study which involved fieldwork in eight schools over a two-year period from 2001 to 2002. Three of these schools were primary schools, all on the East coast of Ireland. In the three primary schools, interviews were conducted with key staff including teachers, principals and a total of 132 children of different nationalities (including 'Irish'). Within the primary schools, both younger and older children were interviewed, generally in friendship groups of four or five children. Intensive qualitative research was conducted in one primary school. The original report of this study (Devine and Kelly, 2002) is divided into two main sections which look at the views of teachers and the experiences of children respectively.

Some of the key findings from the teachers were as follows:

- Although not the norm, erratic enrolment and attendance by some ethnic minority pupils caused a lot of strain for teachers and schools.

- Teachers felt that there was insufficient information and resources available for coping with changes related to immigration and multi-culturalism.

- Contact with minority parents was difficult to sustain, and such contact as existed could be challenging because of cultural differences in child-rearing practices (especially the use of corporal punishment and expectations regarding children's school and home 'duties').

- Although some teachers began from a position of wariness of migrant children, these views tended to become more positive over time, and most teachers spoke in warm terms about their experiences with minority children, in particular what they perceived as their impressive work ethic and respect for authority.

- Teachers noted that a tendency towards inter-ethnic integration in children's friendship groups was evident at primary school level. However, concern was expressed about a lack of integration outside of school hours.

- Teachers were also aware of ethnic tensions between children in their schools but were unsure as to the nature and extent of any problem.

- Teachers appeared to favour the promotion of belonging rather than distinctiveness among students; the former they felt was better achieved through averting discussions on racism. Similarly, while some teachers were aware of the need for cultural recognition, most spoke in terms of the need to absorb into the majority culture of the school.

Some of the key relevant findings from research with the children were as follows:

- For majority children, interaction with young people from different ethnic backgrounds was analysed in terms of fluctuations along a continuum of inclusion and exclusion (e.g. sharing common interests) that is part and parcel of the dynamics of children's social worlds.

- However, cutting across such patterns of interaction were issues to do with difference/sameness, with children who are perceived as being different (for example, derived from their ethnic identity, skin colour, dress etc.) often struggling to include themselves and be included in friendship groups.

- Barriers identified by majority children to the formation of friendships with immigrant children related to language differences, as well as a perceived shyness/quietness on the part of many immigrant children.

- Some children from minority ethnic groups proudly asserted their ethnic identity and cultural difference, while others tried to minimise them.

- Most children (both minority and majority ethnic) did not identify racism and/or hostile attitudes to minority ethnic children as a major problem in school. However, minority children of all ages recounted incidents of racist abuse in their out-of-school lives.

- Most children had at their disposal a repertoire of racially abusive terms which they had both used and observed to be used in the course of their school lives.

- Primary school children indicated that name-calling in relation to skin colour and Traveller status were the 'meanest' forms of name-calling which could be engaged in.

- Name-calling took place predominantly in the 'back stage' regions of school life – in the corridors, toilets, canteens and schoolyards out of view and hearing of teachers. Going to and from school was also identified as a 'site' of such abuse.

The research conducted for the 'Ethnicity and Schooling' report has also been used as the basis for a number of academic articles which present a more theoretical analysis of the findings of this research. Devine (2005) is based on the interviews conducted with both primary and secondary school teachers and analyses how they talk about immigration. Teachers from all schools appeared to struggle with the challenges brought by migration and expressed uncertainty about how to cope. They felt they operated in a policy vacuum and that 'their practice was very much informed by their willingness to identify and seek out initiatives in use elsewhere' (Devine, 2005: 59). Furthermore, while teachers rarely drew attention to racism as an issue, the author argues that conceptions of 'Irishness' and 'Other' often underpinned their discussions, a conceptualisation which is a reflection of that underlying State policy.

Devine and Kelly (2006) focus on the results from the one primary school which received intensive study. They note that among majority children there was a clear idea of what it meant to be 'Irish' (white, settled, Catholic) and migrant children were clearly outside of this. Sporting ability had a significant impact on the level of interaction and status of ethnic minority boys. However, it was noted that this was a double-edged sword as these boys could be subject to racial abuse on the sports field when tensions were high. Ability in the academic sphere could also be helpful in negotiating entry to peer groups. Among the girls, a slightly different pattern emerged but, again, sharing common interests was important for forming and maintaining friendships. The authors draw attention to the fact that the dynamics of social exclusion could work as much within social groups as between them.

Devine, Kenny and Macneela (2008) draw on data from all three primary schools which took part in the research. The article explores how constructions of minority ethnic groups are located within a context that defines what it is to be Irish, including assumptions about skin colour, lifestyle, language and religious belief. The authors conclude that ethnic identity is very significant for negotiating access to peer groups, and discuss the way in which some children use racist name-calling to assert their status. The experience of racist abuse outside of school also appeared to be quite common for minority children. The article also notes that majority children tend to discuss racism solely in terms of skin colour, while minority children (including Traveller children) were 'able to recount their own experiences of being racially abused for colour and/or culturally-based differences'. Some majority children also appeared to show concerns about reverse-racism, feeling that minority children could unfairly exhibit one-upmanship on the basis of superior academic performance.

Devine (2009) draws on the data from the study of the three primary schools, as well as some continuing fieldwork by the author in the intensive case study school. The paper discusses the way in which migrant young people mobilise social and cultural capital, strategically orientating themselves to their primary schooling in order to maximise the exchange value of their education.

This represents a detailed, important body of work and we look forward to the publication of Dympna Devine's forthcoming book (Devine, 2011).

The Dublin 15 study

McGorman and Sugrue (2007) produced an intensive case study of the post-migration challenges primary schools face in the postal district Dublin 15, an area of West Dublin profoundly affected by the new waves of immigration. The initiative for the research was generated locally, born out of frustration by school principals at the new realities they had to face with little assistance. Although the originators of the study warmly appreciated the many positives that multi-culturalism had brought to their schools and district, they felt that there was a profound lack of awareness of the 'rapidly changing multi-cultural environments in which these schools are situated and expected to function'. Fieldwork for the study was conducted from early to mid-2007, and a total 25 primary schools participated. The data for the study included:

- Official statistics from the Census and Department of Education
- Focus group interviews with teachers from different segments of the school curriculum
- Seven case studies with parents from different cultures and ethnic groups
- One focus group interview with primary school pupils
- One focus group interview with Home School Community Liaison teachers.

Statistical evidence showed the extent of changes in Dublin 15 area. From the focus group with teachers, the authors noted the following:

- The level of motivation of newcomer children, who brought with them a desire to work hard, to learn and to succeed, was having a very positive effect in many schools.
- Newcomer children were doing well in academic areas in which English was not a requirement. Because of greater linguistic competence, some were also excelling at Gaeilge.
- Local children were seen as having greater awareness of other cultures and nationalities than they had in the past.
- There was perceived to be a shortage of after-school activities, particularly in newly developing areas, where groups such as the scouts and sports clubs were only in their infancy and were hugely over-subscribed.

- Individual schools have been proactive in adapting to changing realities, but were doing so mostly on an *ad hoc* basis.

This research also found that children did not find racism to be a serious problem inside of school. However, we should treat this finding with extreme caution as it was based on a very small number of children talking in a group setting.

Adapting to Diversity

Adapting to Diversity (Smyth, Darmody, McGinnity and Byrne, 2009), undertaken by the Economic and Social Research Institute and funded by the Department of Education and Science, looked at both primary and secondary schools. We will only review the research conducted in primary schools which consisted of two major components: a survey of school principals and qualitative research in six primary schools. Some of the key findings from the national survey of 746 primary school principals are:

- The majority of primary school principals rate newcomer students as having 'Average' or similar academic achievement to Irish students, while 14 per cent rate them as 'Above average'.

- The majority of primary school principals perceive newcomer students as having 'Above average' or 'Average' motivation in relation to their schoolwork compared to Irish students. Only a small proportion (3 per cent) perceive newcomer students as below average in this respect.

- Over half of both primary and second-level principals reported language difficulties among 'Nearly all' or 'More than half' of their students. Only about one-quarter reported difficulties among 'Only a few' students.

- At both primary and secondary level most school principals see social difficulties as confined to a minority of newcomer students. At primary level, 19 per cent of principals with newcomer students reported that 'Nearly all' or 'More than half' of the newcomer students experience difficulties in social interaction with peers.

- Schools with high proportions of newcomers were somewhat less likely to report good relations between Irish and newcomer students than those with low or medium proportions.

- Bullying and racism were mentioned as contributing 'A lot' or 'Quite a lot' to difficulties among newcomer students by only 8 per cent of principals in primary schools. The authors are careful to note, however, that this is the perspective of principals and some incidents of bullying/racism may not be reported to school staff.

The qualitative element of this research involved interviews with key personnel (language support teachers, classroom teachers and principals) and focus group interviews with (mostly older) children in six primary schools. In total, 258 newcomer and Irish young people, from both primary and secondary schools, took part in these focus groups. Some key relevant findings from the qualitative elements of this project were as follows:

- Newcomer students find most Irish students and teachers friendly.

- The majority of the Irish students interviewed expressed positive views about the number of newcomers coming to Ireland and felt that it made Ireland a more diverse society and allowed exposure to different cultures. However, some students expressed more negative views about the potential impact of immigration on employment and working conditions.

- Sports and other social activities were seen as providing a way to get to know their classmates and 'break the ice'.

- Both teachers and students commented on some difficulties within the social sphere. Newcomers are often seen as socialising among themselves with some reporting difficulties in making Irish friends.

- Poor English can act as a powerful barrier to social interaction and to settling in. Even with good English, accent and slang could pose problems.

- Some newcomers had experienced bullying on the grounds of nationality or ethnicity.

- Primary school students were more likely to say they would approach a teacher if they had been bullied than secondary school pupils. In other cases, however, informing teachers about bullying was seen as escalating rather than reducing potential difficulties.

- In two schools located in a working-class area, students distinguished between a lack of racism in the school and racist behaviour in the local neighbourhood.

The authors note that differences between the teachers'/principals' observations and those of the children may mean that teachers/principals may be unaware of the extent of racist bullying.

Tell Me about Yourself

Tell Me about Yourself (Ni Laoire, Bushin, Carpena-Mendez and White, 2009) used a mixture of qualitative research methods with 194 migrant children (84 boys and 110 girls) from locations around the country (majority from Dublin and the South West). This study is different from those we have looked at so far in a number of ways:

- The design only included migrant children. No adults or local children were interviewed in the study.

- Children were aged 3 to 18 years.

- It was not exclusively school-based but was also conducted in homes, youth clubs, cafes and an asylum accommodation centre.

- It was quite broad in the areas it covered, looking at all aspects of life.
- As well as migrants from Central and Eastern Europe, Latin America and Africa, the study also included children in returning Irish families and children in families which were seeking asylum.

In short, the study systematically included migrant children from different national backgrounds and age groups, with different legal status, and recruited through many different avenues. Some of the key findings were:

- Migrant children are not a homogenous group. They have very different experiences influenced by the complex nature of migration and citizenship rules, social class, ethnicity and motivations for migration. The experience of being a migrant child is thus contingent on many factors.
- Children's lives and opportunities are profoundly affected by their legal status, such that status as migrants can take precedence over status as children. Experiences can vary from the relative comfort of many returning Irish families to the many difficulties experienced by those in the Direct Provision system.[2]
- Migrant children are affected by many issues that affect other children – poor recreational facilities, lack of resourcing for the education system, living in disadvantaged neighbourhoods – but these issues can affect migrant children disproportionately.
- Many migrant children emphasise their similarity with their peers and underplay differences. Others, especially those who are more culturally similar (e.g. on the basis on skin colour or religion), emphasise their differences.

---

[2] Since 2000, all asylum seekers are required to live in state-sponsored accommodation centres. While in 'Direct Provision', asylum seekers receive full board and an allowance of €19.60 per week. They may not work.

- Views which represent children as either inherently vulnerable victims or inherently adaptable are extremes. Children in this research were found to encounter difficulties, but also to be capable of adopting complex trans-cultural competencies and strategies for coping with migration. Many children feel that migration has been beneficial for them.
- Even short-term separations from family, caused by both state policy and family decision making over which they have little control, can be difficult for children.

Other relevant studies

A number of studies not looking directly at the social implications of cultural diversity among children can provide us with further important pieces of evidence. *Moving Up: The Experiences of First-Year Students in Post-primary Education* (Smyth, McCoy and Darmody, 2004) is an ESRI study of the transition from primary school into the first year of secondary school based on a postal survey of 567 school principals and case study analysis in 12 schools. Although the main focus of the study was on the academic and social aspects of transition, the study also indicated that a greater proportion of 'non-national' students had experienced bullying. In order, the most frequent forms of bullying reported by 'non-national' students were being 'Jeered', 'Upset by things said', 'Ignored' and 'Physically pushed'.

The Irish component of the Health Behaviour in School-aged Children study (HBSC) collects data on health, diet, physical activity and substance use but also on fighting, bullying and peer interaction. A separate analysis of the data (Molcho, Kelly, Gavin and Nic Gabhainn, 2008) specifically looked at differences between Travellers, immigrants, disabled and chronically ill pupils and students in the Department of Education and Science's School Support Programme for disadvantaged schools, Delivering Equality of Opportunity in Schools (DEIS). Students in each of these groups were matched with a sub-group from the national sample matched for age, gender, social class and location. The sample for the study was largely taken from secondary schools, but approximately 13 per cent were taken from primary fifth and sixth classes. Unfortunately, the analysis does not allow us to separate the findings for this primary school group. Some findings of relevance to the present study are that:

- Immigrant students were less likely to report feeling very happy with their lives at present compared to their matched group.
- Non-UK immigrant students were less likely to report drinking alcohol or history of drunkenness, although this finding was statistically significant only for boys. Non-UK immigrant students were also less likely to report that they were current smokers compared to their matched group.
- More immigrant students reported that they participated in exercise less than once a week and fewer reported that they were physically active five days or more in the last week.
- Immigrant students were more likely to report that they had been bullied in school in the past couple of months. However, no differences were evident between immigrant students and their matched group in relation to involvement in bullying others, or fighting, or in reporting a medically attended injury.
- Non-UK immigrant students were less likely to report that students in their classes accept them as they are, that they spend three or more evenings with friends or that they have three or more same-sex friends.

A survey study entitled 'Well-being of Children, Families and Neighbourhoods' was commissioned by a number of Irish NGOs and looked at well-being of children and adults in a select number of locations in and around Dublin between 2007 and 2008. A later analysis focused only on the data collected in one disadvantaged area of South Dublin city known as 'The Liberties' and looked at differences between immigrant and local participants (Fanning, Haase and O'Boyle, 2011). The study found that migrants had comparatively higher levels of education and were more likely to be in full-time employment. Of particular relevance for the present study, they found that compared to local children immigrant children reported very few conduct problems, emotional symptoms, hyperactivity, peer problems or anti-social behaviour. They also found that immigrant parents were more optimistic about the educational prospects of their children.

The research we have just reviewed represents all the major research evidence we could locate on social interaction between migrant and local Irish children in primary schools. The majority of the work has been qualitative, looking in-depth at a small number of sites. The available survey data is valuable but largely incidental or collected from secondary sources (e.g. school principals).[3] Each piece of the available evidence may be thought of as a fragment which gives us a momentary and partial window on a rich and complex social world, a child's world not open to easy adult inspection, a world which involves a densely layered, cultural, ethnic and social mix.

A New Study

The main body of this book is given over to reporting the results from an intensive qualitative study conducted in seven schools in Dublin's inner-city. Before going into greater depth in the following chapters, we will briefly outline the distinctive features of the research study presented in this book:

- This research is firmly committed to consistently accessing and articulating the perspective of children. This means doing all we could to ensure that children felt comfortable with the research process and choosing methodologies and approaches to data analysis that represent fairly the micro-dynamics of their social world and allow their voices to be heard as directly as possible. The aim was to penetrate the social world of children using the classroom as a base but looking at many areas outside of school. To adult eyes the social world of

---

[3] Collecting in-depth survey data on these issues is a challenge, an issue we will return to in the last chapter.

children is a subterranean one, a complex world that most of us are still dimly aware of but find difficult to bring to consciousness. It is a world of cliques, games, rules, norms, favourite TV shows and sport stars, where who plays with whom is gossip and where there are strong but fluctuating boundaries separating playmates, best friends and a variety of other groups. We believe very strongly that approaching these issues firmly committed to the perspective of the child yields very important insights into the realities of social interaction between children in multi-cultural situations, and what might be done to maximise the benefits and reduce the risks of such environments.

- This research was based on a detailed examination of the micro-dynamics of the interaction between children.

- The present study is a case study of a site which has received little specific attention to date in relation to these issues. Dublin's north inner-city is a site of great demographic and historical interest. It is an area which houses long settled, economically disadvantaged communities. It is also one of the areas nationally which has experienced the greatest demographic change as a result of the increase in inward migration.

- As well as interviews, the research involved observation in the classroom and school yard, and classroom activities with all children who took part. This meant that, in general, it was possible to build rapport and shared experience between the interviewer and the child prior to the actual interview.

This research examines the views and experiences of both migrant and local Irish young people. Because the unit of analysis is the classroom as well as the individual (every child in a particular class was interviewed) it was possible to examine directly how the experiences of migrant and local children relate to one another.

Chapter 2

A Case Study in North Inner-City Dublin[*]

In this chapter we discuss the nature of case study research as a tool for the in-depth study of particular contexts. We then present some background material on the area in which this research took place, north inner-city Dublin. In this context we also discuss the results of a survey we conducted in this area in 2007 and repeated in 2008.

As a form of research, case studies place great emphasis on the importance of the context in which social phenomena occur. They focus on the circumstances and complexities of a single case or small number of cases (Bowling, 2002). If we take, as a hypothetical example, a case study researcher studying a school, they will generally collect information using a variety of methods from a range of sources to produce an intensive analysis which tells the story of *that* school. This distinctive feature of case study research emerges with greater clarity when multiple cases or schools are involved. In such situations, the researcher studies each school intensively, following the same basic procedure and using multiple methods and multiple sources before compiling an analysis of each school separately. Only when each individual case has been understood on its own terms is any form of generalisation (called *cross-case analysis*) attempted (Creswell, 1998). Case studies produce detailed accounts of how phenomena work in everyday life and are ideal for the study of complex social

---

[*] This chapter was authored by Philip Curry, Robbie Gilligan and Derek Murphy.

settings (Bowling, 2004). Case studies are not designed to be statistically representative but to explore in depth how phenolmena work and why. Case studies are widely used in some disciplines (e.g. Business Studies, Clinical Psychology), but have a long history in most forms of social research (Yin, 2008).

The current research involved a detailed study of a single case. It aims to analyse social interaction between children in one historically and demographical distinct area: north inner-city Dublin. The advantages of a case study approach for the present research are:

- The social world of children is complex and often difficult to access for adults. Intensive qualitative research methods with multiple forms of data collection are ideal for reliably accessing that world.

- As outlined in the previous chapter, migration into Ireland has been a remarkably complex affair with migrants coming from many different parts of the world. Large scale migration has also happened recently and rapidly. Intensive research is suitable for capturing the rapidly changing, emerging and complex realities involved.

- Contextual factors play hugely important roles in the lives of schools and communities.

We should of course bear in mind one important qualification: case studies are not and do not claim to be representative. The way in which conclusions from one case study site are extended to another is by means of replication and comparison, not by direct transplantation. Where possible, we will attempt to relate the findings from our case study to findings from other sites. More generally, we believe that the findings from our case study are relevant to other contexts but that it requires some work to explore those other contexts and then draw out the meaning of similarities and differences in terms of the findings presented here.

Dublin North Inner-City

North inner-city Dublin (the Northside) is not an official administrative area but a term that is increasingly used to refer to the area north of the river Liffey, roughly bounded on the east by the Grand Canal and on the west by the Phoenix Park. For the purpose of the study, we defined the north inner-city as a slightly larger area corresponding to Dublin postal codes 1, 3 and 7, an area extending from East Wall to Stoneybatter.

The north inner-city has long been associated with deprivation. The 'Monto', Dublin's red light district and situated in the area, closed in the 1920s and was the subject of a playful song by The Dubliners folk group in the 1960s. The actual reality was no laughing matter. Prostitution – and poverty – were serious threats to public health. The death rate from venereal disease in Dublin in 1916 was almost twice the rate for London and close to three times that for Belfast (Luddy, 2007). Thirty-five years earlier, a colonel commanding a British regiment based in Dublin had testified that over 43 per cent of his men who were not married had been incapacitated for duty due to venereal disease (Prunty, 1999). The picture of ill health more generally was even bleaker, thanks largely to unsanitary conditions. Death rates for Dublin in 1871 were 36 per 1,000 population, compared to rates of 24 for London, 22 for Glasgow or 21 for Edinburgh (Prunty, 1999).

Economically, the area has long been in decline with local jobs disappearing due to impact of economic and social change. Both the number of jobs and population fell due to the mechanisation of the docks in the 1960s, and the drift of industry and business to the suburbs. Most of the 311 derelict sites in the city in 1978 were located within the canal ring – and mostly on the north side (Bannon, Eustace and O'Neill, 1981). Inevitably, in the face of this economic decline, the population of the overall inner-city fell by half in the period 1961–1991. On the education front, the evidence was equally bleak. A study done in 1970 found that only 3 per cent of parents in the area had passed the primary certificate examination (Carney et al., 1970), a largely routine step for most Irish children living outside the area. The primary certificate was then an important point of transition, in the days before free secondary education was introduced by Donough O'Malley TD, a Fianna Fáil Minister for Education, in 1966. In those pre-free education days, a limited scholarship scheme was the only route by which poorer children could aspire to secondary education.

What threw the deprivation of the area into sharp relief was that it existed cheek by jowl with the privilege enjoyed by those from the wider city. Ironically, in an area suffering huge educational deprivation could be found some of the most famous secondary schools in the country: Belvedere College, Loreto North Great Georges Street, Dominican Eccles Street, O'Connells Schools and Colaiste Mhuire, Parnell Street. Of these, three are closed and have transferred to the suburbs, one serves a more local catchment area, and one (Belvedere) largely retains its original role.

The area has changed considerably since the economic boom of the 1990s with rising property prices and many large-scale property developments changing the demographic profile of the area in places. Community groups in the area have begun to refer to Dublin's inner-city as a 'Divided City', and a densely knit patchwork of extreme affluence and deprivation (Haase and Byrne; 2007).

Another major change affecting the area has been migration. The north inner-city has anecdotally been seen as the first port of call for many newly arrived migrants, offering relatively affordable housing, adjacent to employment opportunities and good transport infrastructure. Of course, the area also poses many challenges for migrants, especially families, with comparatively high crime and unemployment rates.

In the next section we attempt to present some sense of the scale of the impact which these changes have had on the educational system in the area.

School Composition in North Inner-City: The NICSS Surveys

An early strand of the current research project was the documentation of the demographic composition of schools in the area. This took the form of the North Inner-City Schools Survey (NICSS) which was launched in April 2007.

The NICSS set out to collect data on all students in all public, non-specialised primary schools within a defined area of Dublin's north inner-city. In total, there are 17 schools in the area, most being DEIS schools.[†] The survey asked every teacher in the participating schools to provide the following information on pupils in their class:

- Age
- Gender
- Nationality
- Proficiency in English
- Date of first enrolment
- Area of residence
- Mode of transport to and from school.

The teacher was required to record this information individually for all children in their class. Data entry was thus quite onerous on the teachers and we again wish to express our gratitude for their participation.

The North Inner-City School Survey was conducted in April 2007 and April 2008. In 2007, all schools (17) in the area took part and in 2008, all but one (16) took part. In 2007, data was collected on 2,786 pupils, and in 2008 on 2,676 pupils. As we wish to compare the results over the two waves of NICSS, the results presented here pertain only to those 16 schools which participated in both years.

[†] Delivering Equality of Opportunity is an initiative by the Department of Education and Skills 'designed to ensure that the most disadvantaged schools benefit from a comprehensive package of supports, while ensuring that others continue to get support in line with the level of disadvantage among their pupils' (Department of Education and Skills, 2010).

We can see from Table 3 that between 2007 and 2008 the number of migrant pupils attending schools in the inner-city increased slightly, but over both years it remained reasonably stable at just over 30 per cent.

Table 3: Number of migrant pupils attending north inner-city primary schools, 2007 and 2008

	2007	2008
'Old Irish'	1,792 (68.5%)	1,755 (65.6%)
Migrant	824 (31.5%)	921 (34.4%)
Total	2,616 (100%)	2,676 (100%)

The NICSS data also reveals the enormous diversity of nationalities attending schools in the north inner-city. The surveys recorded 56 different national backgrounds (including Irish) with the four most frequent being 'Old' Irish, Romanian background, Nigerian background and Polish background.

As can be seen from Table 4, however, no one group dominates and there are pupils from many different countries, including many nationalities which are represented by less than 10 pupils.

Although there were clear differences between individual schools, on aggregate there was a strong trend for Junior classes to have higher concentrations of migrants. This trend increased slightly between 2007 and 2008 (Table 5). It is noticeable that by 2008, primary schools in the inner-city had on average over 50 per cent migrant pupils in Junior and Senior Infant classes.

Table 4: *Frequency and Percentage of Different Nationality Groups, 2007 and 2008*

	2007 Frequency	2007 %	2008 Frequency	2008 %
Romanian	148	18.0%	186	20.2%
Nigerian	112	13.6%	76	8.3%
Identified as 'Migrant'**	115	14.0%	0	0.0%
Polish	82	10.0%	85	9.2%
Filipino	47	5.7%	49	5.3%
Slovakian	32	3.9%	38	4.1%
Lithuanian	34	4.1%	32	3.5%
'Other'	35	4.2%	26	2.8%
Romanian/Irish-born	24	2.9%	53	5.8%
Chinese	18	2.2%	25	2.7%
Indian	16	1.9%	23	2.5%
Nigerian/Irish-born	17	2.1%	50	5.4%
Latvian	16	1.9%	16	1.7%
Mauritian	14	1.7%	31	3.4%
Georgian	14	1.7%	13	1.4%
South African	13	1.6%	10	1.1%
Mongolian	11	1.3%	17	1.8%
Bulgarian	11	1.3%	12	1.3%
Countries with less than 10 in either year	42	5.1%	125	13.6%
Missing	23	2.8%	54	5.9%
Total	**824**	**100.0**	**921**	**100.0**

** In the first year of the survey some schools were reluctant to provide more detailed information about the characteristics of their pupils.

Table 5: Percentage of migrant pupils in each class in School, 2007 and 2008

	2007	2008
Junior infants	52.1%	58.5%
Senior infants	48.1%	54.4%
1st class	28.7%	49.0%
2nd class	23.8%	26.2%
3rd class	19.7%	31.1%
4th class	18.3%	27.8%
5th class	26.5%	23.9%
6th class	14.4%	28.3%

We can also see from the table above that the cohorts which in 2007 were in Junior and Senior Infants appeared to move into Senior Infants and First class respectively in 2008. This stability is reflected in the fact that between 2007 and 2008 the average length of enrolment for all migrant pupils increased from 16.3 months (S.D: 14.3) to 20.4 months (S.D: 17.55).

There were also remarkable differences between individual schools in the percentage of migrant pupils attending. In 2008, the percentage of migrant pupils attending these primary schools varied between a high of 60.4 per cent and a low of 4.0 per cent, and within these limits there were very large differences between individual schools (Table 6).

In both years of the NICSS survey, migrant children were slightly more likely to live outside the area of the school they were attending, however differences in this regard were slight and the vast majority of migrant pupils lived in the NICSS area. In 2007, 1,593 (95.2 per cent) of the Irish children were recorded as residing in the general area covered by the NICSS survey, while 737 (91.5 per cent) of the migrant children did so. In 2008, 1,400 (95.1 per cent) of the Irish children were living in the NICSS area, while 792 (88.2 per cent) of the migrant children did so.

Table 6: Percentage of migrant pupils by individual school, 2008

	Per Cent Migrant
School 1	4.0%
School 2	6.4%
School 3	19.7%
School 4	20.7%
School 5	23.2%
School 6	32.2%
School 7	33.5%
School 8	33.9%
School 9	34.7%
School 10	37.1%
School 11	44.7%
School 12	48.0%
School 13	55.6%
School 14	60.4%

Note: There are only fourteen schools listed, as for the purpose of this table, three Junior schools (Junior and Senior Infants, First class) have been combined with the primary schools they feed into.

Although migrant children were largely living within the area in which NICSS was centred, they were almost twice as likely as Old Irish children to reside outside of it in 2007. This difference increased substantially in 2008. Whereas 1.7 per cent of the Irish students were recorded as living in 'other areas', this was the case for 8.9 per cent of migrant children.

Eleven principals were asked to rate the social interaction of Irish and migrant children in their schools on a scale from 1 = 'Very poor' to 10 = 'Very good'. Their ratings were generally very positive. All principals rated interaction as 5 or higher, and only one gave a rating lower than a 7. Seven principals rated interaction as 8, 9 or 10.

Discussion

The survey data just presented shows that the schools, and by implication the communities, of north inner-city Dublin have been profoundly affected by migration. Between 2007 and 2008, the percentage of migrant pupils in primary schools in the area remained relatively stable at just over 30 per cent. This is over three times the national average of 10 per cent migrant pupils in primary schools (Smith, Darmody, McGinnity and Byrne, 2009). What these numbers represent for schools can only be appreciated when we examine the statistics in more detail and see that the percentage of migrants is highly concentrated in Junior years and in certain schools.

Smyth, Darmody, McGinnity and Byrne (2009) also found that many newcomer students tend to be highly concentrated in certain primary schools: many (four in ten) had no newcomer children at all while a small number (one-tenth) had more than one-fifth of their student population made up of newcomer students. The authors cite availability of places in schools, residential patterns and enrolment policies ('first come, first served'; priority given to siblings) as causes of this pattern.

The NICSS focused on a very narrow, relatively homogenous geographic area which makes the variation in numbers more striking. Some of the schools at the lower and higher end of the concentration spectrum shown in Table 6 are within ten minutes walking distance of one another. Residential patterns, therefore, appear to play a small part in the huge differences observed in the percentage of migrants present in different schools. The disparities in this regard are yet to be explained fully, but for now we can note that on superficial inspection there are no obvious differences to distinguish between the schools with high and low concentrations of migrants. Among educators we have spoken to in the area, there seems to be a certain acquiescence about these differences, but the scale of the disparities so soon after the advent of large-scale migration to Ireland may bode ill for the future of social integration among children in the inner-city.

Chapter 3

Entering the Social World of Children

In this chapter we discuss how the child-centred methodology of the study was developed and why it included child-friendly research techniques such as participant observation and interviews in groups of two or three. We also look at how we selected sites to work in and how the research was arranged to respect the ethical rights of schools, children and their parents. Finally, we look at some findings from the present research, which illustrate one important lesson from the use of child-centred methods: things can happen within the child's social sphere of which adults very close to them such as teachers and parents are largely unaware. This finding is substantiated by other findings from Irish and international research. The chapter concludes with a discussion of the implications for research methodology and policy regarding ethnic relations among school children.

This study is based on the view that children's social relationships and cultures are worthy of study in their own right, independently of the perspectives and concerns of adults (James and Prout, 1997). We therefore adopted a child-centred approach which shows respect for children, acknowledges their competencies and capacities and promotes the entitlement of children to be considered persons of value with rights and responsibilities (Greene and Hill, 2005). Such an approach is not only desirable in its own right, but is also the ideal ethos for a study which aims to penetrate into the social world of children, the sphere in which children interact freely with one another outside of adult supervision. It is of course a mistake to think of this as a separate physical sphere; it is a social arena defined by its own norms and history, woven seamlessly into the fabric of the social life of children.

School is a crucial site for social interaction for children, particularly among migrant children. The separate social world of children can emerge within the school context as soon as an adult presence is absent, whether for an extended period during break time or momentarily when the teacher's back is turned. Below is a short example taken from the present research, in which some children talk about who they do and do not play with. It has nothing directly to do with inter-ethnic relations, but is a brief example of the politics of social relations which occur among children in primary schools:

> *Girl 1*: I don't play chasing because you play with Mary Murphy and all.
>
> *Inter*: Okay, so Alice, you don't play with these two in the yard, why not?
>
> *Girl 1*: They play with other girls that I don't like.
>
> *Inter*: And who do you play with now?
>
> *Girl 1* [*Ignoring question*]: I don't like Sarah or Deirdre ...
>
> *Girl 2*: Well you used to like them ...
>
> *P4/137, Local girls, Fourth class, School 6*

Stories of shifting alliances such as these – gossip about who is now playing with whom, and who is good at what – are important elements of interaction among children that we must take seriously when talking to them and trying to understand their social world.

In short, the aim of this research is to document how children interact among themselves. On a methodological level, accessing the social world of children presents a challenge. It requires the use of a flexible range of techniques and the modification of traditional ones to accommodate the different life experiences and abilities of children (Punch, 2002a).

Selecting Schools and Classes

Although the present study is not an educational one *per se*, we decided to use schools as research sites for a number of reasons:

- Anecdotal evidence suggested that migrant and local Irish children interacted very little outside of school settings. Our subsequent research experience strongly confirmed this view.
- Practically all children attend primary school of some sort. Schools, therefore, do not suffer from any of the selection biases which would result from using non-school sites such as community groups or sports teams.

The aim of this research was to gain insight into key issues and dimensions of inter-ethnic relations among primary school children in the north inner-city Dublin area. In order to do this we aimed to work in as diverse a range of schools as possible. We did this using *maximum variation sampling*, an approach in qualitative research used to select sites or participants in such a way as to guarantee the greatest amount of possible diversity. The NICSS data was used as the basis of site selection. We selected two all girls' schools, two all boys' schools and three mixed schools. Within each of these groups we selected schools which had different ethnic compositions. We also tried to select schools which had different concentrations of migrants, but we excluded those which had less than 8 per cent migrants on their rolls, as the aim was to study social interaction and not just attitudes.

We also wanted to ensure a good geographical spread through the north inner-city area. This was achieved fortuitously when we had selected on the basis above.

A lesson that we learnt early in the first pilot study was that classrooms provided the preferred research unit. This meant that any and every research activity that we engaged in within a school would be offered to every member of a particular class.

Children were very eager to take part, and selecting some children to be involved and not others would have left many feeling excluded from the study. We therefore felt that, in the interests of fair representation, it was important to give everybody the chance to be interviewed (see Hill et al., 2006). This greatly increased the number of interviews we had to conduct, but we still felt this approach was preferable. It also had the added value that the data we collected forms a very comprehensive account of social life in participating classrooms. In selecting classes, we aimed to ensure that we covered a broad range of ages so in each school we initially sought to work with one Second, one Fourth and one Sixth class. This had to be adjusted to suit the needs of some schools, but the basic principle remained the same. For example, in one school we worked in First, Fourth and Sixth classes.

Seven primary schools participated in the research. In one school, four classes took part and in two others only two classes took part. Hence, a total of 20 classrooms participated in the research. Only one school that we approached refused to participate. The reason given was that it was late in the year and they had commitments to take part in other research.

All of the schools served largely working class neighbourhoods. Four of the seven were part of the Department of Education's Delivering Equality of Opportunity in Schools (DEIS) programme which is 'designed to ensure that the most disadvantaged schools benefit from a comprehensive package of supports' (Department of Education, 2010). Like many primary schools in Ireland, these schools were relatively small, predominately serving their local area.

Five of the seven participating schools had between 170 and 220 pupils. The two others were larger schools having 293 and 364 respectively. Table 7 gives further details about the characteristics of the schools taking part. The total number of pupils in each school is not shown in this table as they would be too easy to identify in an area the size of Dublin's north inner-city.

Table 7: Characteristics of the Schools Taking Part in the Research

	Gender Composition of School	Per Cent Migrant Children in School	Classes Taking Part	Number of Participants	DEIS School
School 1	Mixed	33.5%	Two Senior Infants, Fourth and Fifth	73	DEIS school
School 2	Mixed	44.7%	Second, Fourth and Sixth	53	Not DEIS school
School 3	Mixed	19.7%	First, Fourth and Sixth	45	DEIS school
School 4	Boys	34.7%	Second, Fourth and Sixth	46	Not DEIS school
School 5	Boys	23.2%	Second and Sixth	35	DEIS school
School 6	Girls	20.7%	Fourth, Fifth and Sixth	58	Not DEIS school
School 7	Girls	55.6%	Fourth and a combined Fifth and Sixth	33	DEIS school

Thus, a total of two Senior Infant classes, one First class, three Second classes, six Fourth classes, two Fifth classes, one combined Fifth and Sixth class and five Sixth classes took part.

Each school was approached approximately four weeks prior to field work. At this meeting, we sought consent from the principal to invite staff and students in their school to participate. In some cases, the approval of the board of management was also required. We then asked the principal to nominate teachers of classes which they believed met our criteria and to invite those teachers to meet with us. Approximately one week later, we met with interested class teachers to discuss the research. We presented them with written information about the research, explained the purpose of the project and answered any questions. When teachers agreed to participate, we visited the class approximately one week prior to commencing field work there. At this meeting, we explained the research to the children and provided them with age appropriate information and consent forms for themselves and their parents. Teachers then collected both child and parental consent forms prior to the fieldwork commencing. In some instances, we had to secure the child's consent on the first day of fieldwork. In the small number of cases in which child or parental consent was missing, we still conducted research in that class but did not interview the child and excluded all data which referred to them from our analysis.

The fact that consent was voluntary and could be withdrawn at any time was reiterated throughout the project. In addition, researchers paid particular attention to the children's assent to being involved in the research process based on a constant awareness of their responses to the researchers' presence. Cocks (2006) argues that this method of constantly negotiating the willingness of children to be involved in the process is particularly useful when conducting research with children for whom language is problematic.

The Children

In total, 343 children were interviewed along with ten teachers. A total of 206 (60.1 per cent) of these children were girls and 137 (39.9 per cent) were boys. As can be seen from Table 8, the largest numbers of pupils came from Sixth, Fourth and Second classes.

Table 8: Number of participants by year in school

	Frequency	Per Cent
Senior Infants	32	9.3%
First Class	23	6.7%
Second Class	63	18.4%
Fourth Class	89	25.9%
Fifth Class	45	13.1%
Mixed Fifth and Sixth Class	21	6.1%
Sixth Class	70	20.4%
TOTAL	343	100%

The spilt of Irish and migrant background children was 245 (71.4 per cent) Irish and 98 (28.6 per cent) migrant. The largest groups of migrant children were from Romania (19, 5.5 per cent), Nigeria (15, 4.4 per cent), Poland (11, 3.2 per cent) and Lithuania (6, 1.7 per cent). Smaller numbers came from Albania, Bulgaria, China, Egypt, Philippines, Georgia, Hungry, India, Italy, Kenya, Kosovo, Latvia, Lesotho, Malaysia, Moldavia, Mongolia, Mauritius, Pakistan, Russia, Slovakia, Somalia, South Africa, Turkey, Ukraine, Zambia and Zimbabwe.

Given the large number of participants, we used identification numbers instead of pseudonyms. However, in many interviews participants refer to people by name. In these cases, all names have been replaced by pseudonyms. These were chosen on a non-alliterative basis but matched to traditional national or ethnic group names using a baby name website.

Research Methods

In each school, we tailored methodologies to suit the conditions in the particular site but, in general, research in a participating classroom consisted of a three-week period of observation and interviewing structured as described below.

Week 1

At least four hours of participant observation in the classroom and school yard. The classroom time included at least one formal lesson and one less structured session such as art or PE. As far as possible, a 'least adult' role (Mandell, 1988) was adopted by researchers in order to minimise their status as adults in the school. For example, as far as ethically possible, researchers avoided censuring and disciplining those whom they encountered 'misbehaving'.

Week 2

In the second week we attempted to get to know the children a little better. In the early stages of the research, we experimented with the use of 'research games' such as engaging in an art project (Merriman and Geurin, 2006) with younger children and a photographic project (Punch; 2002b) with older ones. These were directly related to themes of community and ethnic identity. However, we found that these activities added little to research data. Instead, we used more fun 'ice-breaker' games which allowed the researcher and the children to enjoy one another's company and get to know each other better. The second week also included at least four hours of further participant observation in classrooms and in the school yard.

Week 3

Every child in the participating classroom was interviewed once. The children where given a slip of paper which allowed them to elect to be interviewed alone or with one or two friends. The fieldworker then sorted through these preferences and wrote out an interview list, making sure those who wanted to be interviewed alone could do so and those who elected to go with a friend were paired with at a least one of their named friends. The majority of children chose at least one friend to be interviewed with. The largest interviews involved three participants but a minority also involved only one participant.

Interviews were semi-structured and followed an age-appropriate topic guide covering life in the classroom, friendships, life outside of school and a story telling exercise. Interviews were kept conversational, and the children's own terms and descriptive language were used by the interviewers where possible. In the first instance, interviewers referred to migrant children as 'children from other countries'. However, if children used the words 'foreign' or 'foreigner', the interviewer reflected this terminology back to them, in accordance with a least adult role. However racial nicknames were not repeated by the interviewers.

Interviews were also coloured by the participant observation which had taken place prior to the interview. This allowed interviewers to be very direct and concrete in the questions they asked and to engage in detailed discussion of friendship networks with which interviewer and child were familiar. The use of interviews allowed us to understand more fully that which was observed, while the use of observation sometimes allowed us to verify what was said. We occasionally found that children could express generically positive opinions about the value of diversity, while avoiding actual contact with minority children in their class. On occasion, children could also over-represent how much they interacted with minority children. For example, in the following exchange, the child appears to be eager to suggest that they have foreign national friends while the interviewer appears to be less than convinced:

Inter: So, you don't have any friends who are not Irish?

Local girl: Anna.

....

Inter: What about Anna?

Local girl: Ah, she's very nice.

Inter: I never seen her, like you're never with her.

Local girl: She does play with all ... you know, the people who talk her way and all.

P137, Local girl, Fourth class, School 6

Such inconsistencies are part and parcel of the research process, but they do caution us that we cannot take everything we hear at face value. In general, we found that the more time we spent in individual classes the deeper our understanding of the social world of that classroom became.

Professional interpreters who had experience working with children were available as required. The fieldwork was conducted between Christmas and May 2008. For the most part, both migrant and local Irish children were well settled into their school year at this point.

Class teachers were also interviewed. The main purpose of these interviews was to discuss their opinions on the history of friendship networks in their class, but there were some more general questions about how migration had affected the school and their teaching practice. However, the focus of the research was firmly on the child's world, not on teaching practice *per se*. Teachers were provided with written information about the research and signed consent forms.

Teacher Perspectives on the Child's Space in School – An Important Lesson

Our research gave us a very strong sense that teachers engaged with the job of teaching can be unaware of some of the more negative social interaction that goes on 'when their backs are turned'. This can be reinforced by language and cultural barriers between migrant pupils and Irish primary school teachers. We will take two examples to illustrate this point. In one Second year classroom in which we conducted research, the teacher summed up social relations in her classroom as follows:

> Generally they all get on very well. They are typical eight year olds and seven year olds in that, they love telling on each other and that kind of thing but there is nobody who goes out of their way to be mean to anybody else, like they do generally get on very well and you can see that in PE when you say get a group, they just run to anybody, it doesn't have to be their very best friend or anything like that.
>
> *Teacher 1, Second class, School 2*

This teacher also commented that new children tend to settle in quickly:

> They settle quite quickly and I suppose because they are so young they adapt to things quickly whether it is boys from their old school or from the two different ... they kind of mix fairly fast.
>
> *Teacher 1, Second class, School 2*

We might not expect from these comments that the classroom had some of the worst racial bullying of any class that we visited. We will return to some of the children's experiences from this class later. For now, two illustrative comments will suffice:

> People hate me.
>
> *P268, Nigerian boy, Second class, School 2*

> *Nigerian boy*: Because my body is not white.
>
> *Inter*: And do many people make a big deal out of that, do they?
>
> *Nigerian boy*: Yes.
>
> *P339, Nigerian boy, Second class, School 2*

Contradicting the teacher's comments above about settling in quickly, the last child observes:

> Well when you were new they were trying to be extra nice but when I am starting to get used to them they would start hitting me.
>
> *P339, Nigerian boy, Second class, School 2*

By its very nature, the social world of children is far removed from the teacher's knowledge. Teachers are often preoccupied with the practicalities of teaching, especially since these have often been complicated by the arrival of migrant children who bring many differences to the classroom.

We encountered broadly similar phenomena in girls' schools. In one Fourth class, the teacher comments:

> No, like within the group that I have now I don't think there are any sort of race issues.
>
> *Teacher 3, Fourth class, School 3*

In this case, the teacher is aware that she may be being over-optimistic:

> I think overall they get on very well, now I mean children anyway are liable to have their kind of things like that but I think that's down to more, any time that they have a disagreement I think it's really more down to personality rather than a race issue. Now that's really optimistic but I just would think that, I don't think that the children would ever look down on or have a superiority complex because they're Irish and they're children from another country, I don't think that.
>
> *Teacher 3, Fourth class, School 3*

This observation reinforces the basic point that much goes on outside of the teacher's 'ken', and that teachers themselves are aware of this. In this example, we also see a tendency to interpret disagreements as due to 'personality' rather than cultural or ethnic difference. This class was again one in which there were marked problems:

> Yeah, they would take my pen and put it somewhere I won't see and I will have to look for it everywhere. They would splash juice on my face and do like that on my face. When I tidy my bag, my purse jewellery is in my bag with my things, they just take my purse and smell it and do smelly faces.
>
> P112, Mauritian girl, Fourth class, School 3

Bullying and intimidation are by their nature events that pupils will hide from the teacher and there can be a classroom *omertà* culture which operates an honour-based resistance against 'being a rat'. For example, here a child from the same class explains why migrant children in her class do not tell the teacher that they are being picked on:

> *Local girl 1*: But they won't say it to the teacher like.
>
> *Inter*: Yeah. Yeah and why don't you think they say it to the teacher?
>
> *Local girl 1*: Afraid to.
>
> *Local girl 2*: Yeah.
>
> *Inter*: Yeah, they're afraid to, yeah.
>
> P233/286, Local girls, Fourth class, School 3

These kinds of observation are not unique to the present study, but they do have important implications for how we think about research in this area and need to be borne in mind as we try to understand the dynamics of classroom interaction and evaluate different people's perspectives on it.

Discussion

When we think about the aims of education we can be in danger of thinking of the child's social space as an unintended consequence, something that takes place in the hidden corners of the school that could be done away with but for the logistics of teaching different subjects and the human necessity for a break from study (and teaching). However, free time and interaction with peers serve many important functions, such as teaching children independence and important social skills. From the perspective of some children, what goes on within their social space may be more important than what happens in the space they share with adults. What happens there can have a profound impact on the sense of happiness and well-being (or otherwise) of all children.

One important finding in this section of the report is that adults may not be aware of all that happens within the child's social space, particularly bullying, name-calling and other negative behaviours. Previous research on Irish students has indicated that only a small number ever report being bullied to an adult (Smyth et al., 2004). A major national survey conducted in 2008, *Growing Up in Ireland*, involving 8,500 nine-year-olds, their parents and teachers, found that while 40 per cent of nine-year-olds reported being bullied, only 24 per cent of parents reported the same issue (Williams et al., 2009). The present study found that divergent reports between adults and children clearly extend to migrant children and to ethnically motivated bullying and name-calling. Both teachers and parents will often know about friendship groups in which children are or are not involved. However, much of the detail of social interaction between children will go unheeded by adults. We would emphasise that this is as we should expect and it is often something that teachers and parents are very aware of themselves. Interaction with their peers is a crucial element of a child's education and cannot prosper with constant adult supervision. Qualitative research such as this cannot tell us the extent to which the negative experiences of migrant children are likely to be under-reported vis-à-vis those of other children, but differences in language and cultural practice may lead us to suspect that there may be more under-reporting of problematic experiences among migrant children.

We have to be very careful how we understand the fact that teachers may be unaware of much of the negative behaviour that goes on in their classroom. As we have tried to make clear in this chapter, we believe that a certain disparity is an inevitable consequence of the fact that children must be allowed their own social space within and outside of the school environment. As adults, teachers will have limited access to this social space. The teacher's job is a difficult one, especially in rapidly changing circumstances for which they have had little or no training. There may be a temptation to criticise teachers for not being more aware of these issues in their classroom. However, we would argue that is to underestimate the complexities and realities of the situation. Of course, acknowledging these realities and ensuring that teachers receive appropriate training may help improve the situation to a degree, but this is unlikely to happen in a negative atmosphere in which casual criticism is levelled at teachers. The real challenges for adults who are concerned with the more hidden negative interaction that may occur between children in primary school is not how to increase surveillance, but how to condition children to interact constructively with each other when free to do so. Similarly, the mechanisms whereby more serious situations which require adult intervention may be reported are often not immediately obvious to the children. Solutions to these problems are neither obvious nor easy to implement. We will return to the issue of intervention later. For now, let us say that we believe that awareness of the full complexity of the situation, open dialogue and active partnership between all stakeholders will be crucial elements of progress.

Disparities between adult and child perspectives also have important implications for how we conduct research into these issues. The evidence consistently tells us that adult perspectives will tend to underestimate the level of negative behaviour that is occurring. Teachers are often aware of bullying that goes on in and around their school. However, in any given situation we must be open to the possibility that what they know is only the tip of the iceberg. Following on from this, the first point is obvious: the use of adult assessments of the incidence of bullying or other negative behaviour among children should be treated very carefully. In the absence of evidence to the contrary, it must be taken that adults will perceive a more positive picture than actually exists. The point is not that we should not consult adults about their perspectives on these issues, but that we should in no way take adult perspectives on these issues as complete evaluations of what is actually happening. We believe that to do so is detrimental to the interests of vulnerable children. Adult perspectives tell us more about adult perspectives than about the actual world of the child.

The second point is slightly more subtle: can adult perspectives be used to verify children's perspectives? Can we verify what children say by asking adults? In technical research terms this is referred to as triangulation, which basically means cross-checking evidence from different sources. The key question is whether we can triangulate the evidence children give us with what adults tell us? If we are trying to estimate the incidence of bullying or some other negative behaviour, can we assess the views of children, teachers and parents and then by some mechanism arrive at a combined sense of the true incidence? We argue the answer is no. This is something that looks like verification or triangulation because it involves multiple perspectives. However we are 'mixing apples with oranges'. You cannot verify or triangulate by reference to someone who has been encouraged to give their opinions about something about which they may have poor or partial information. Of course, adults will often be correct, but played out over a large scale they may just as often be incorrect. The consequences for vulnerable children can be very harmful as a key aspect of their actual experience may go unrecognised. On the other hand, child reports can be inaccurate and exaggerated. As researchers in this area we are well aware of this. However, key points to bear in mind are:

- In our research we found over-reporting of problems by children not to be very common. Reporting being bullied or called names is something children are generally reluctant to do, so false positives, though they occur, do not occur very often.

- In qualitative research, false reports of bullying and name calling can usually be distinguished quite quickly from true ones.

Our argument then is simple: if we wish to verify or triangulate the self-reports of children, we should do so by reference to sources which can demonstrate reliable access to their social world, for example, direct observation or the evaluation of close peers. To verify or triangulate by reference to the views of adults can be inexpensive and convenient, but it can also risk seriously misrepresenting the experiences of children.

Chapter 4

Migrant and Local Children: Different Languages, Values and Experiences

'School is not cool.'
– *Graffiti on North Strand Road*

As a prelude to looking at how migrant and local children interact, this chapter presents evidence of how the two groups of children often differ from one another. Beyond more obvious differences of language and culture, there are also issues to do with social values, attitudes to education, home life and the very experience of migration itself. We document some of the ways in which these differences can impact on social interaction between migrant and local children. We further argue that the results of this study, taken with other available evidence, provide support for the view that typical migrant families in Ireland are often educated and highly motivated.

Migration is rarely to be understood as a simple movement of people from one society to another. Migrants do not represent a simple cross-section of the society which they leave. For example, they are disproportionately young and single. In the case of migration into Ireland, we also often see that migrants are educated and qualified people who lack opportunities of advancement in the country from which they migrated. These characteristics are often reflected in the expectations for children that migrants bring to, or give birth to, in Ireland.

In this chapter, we will discuss the characteristics of many of the migrant children which we encountered in Dublin's inner-city schools. These children often exhibited many differences from their fellow students, including the experience of migration itself. Many of these issues could form the subject of studies in their own right. For the present, we are most concerned with those that relate to social interaction in the classroom. We will start with language.

The Social Importance of Speaking English

There was an emphatic consensus about the social value of learning English among all the young people and adults to whom we spoke:

> I think you should, if you're a foreign person coming into the country, I think you should just learn the language first and then when you learn it, go over and try to make friends and then you have your friends and you have your language and then you can talk.
>
> – *P295, Local boy, Sixth class, School 4*

> I would say that if they speak the language that is a huge plus because it is easier for the kids to get to know them whereas if they come out with very little English that can be very much an impediment to establishing relationships.
>
> – *Teacher 4, Fifth class, School 6*

> *Inter*: And what do you think, is it easy for you to get on with people from different countries like if they have different languages or anything? Is it easy or is it hard sometimes?
>
> *Nigerian boy*: Hard.
>
> *Inter*: Yeah, why is a bit hard?

> *Nigerian boy*: Because they don't speak the language and it's hard to know what they say.
>
> – *P268, Nigerian boy, Second class, School 2*

> Because if you don't understand they don't respect you.
>
> – *P87, Filipino girl, Fourth class, School 3*

> *Inter*: So how could they make some friends?
>
> *Latvian boy*: Talk English and ask them do you want to be my friend.
>
> – *P128, Latvian boy, First class, School 5*

Having proficient English can therefore be seen as a kind of social capital. Those who do not have English will generally be socially isolated from the rest of the class, sometimes with only a very small number of same language peers to talk to. More likely they will be seen alone in the school yard. Children who speak English can be quite blunt about why they do not bother with children who cannot:

> She doesn't really understand us so what's the point in telling her anything.
>
> – *P239, Local girl, Fourth class, School 6*

> *Inter*: Oh yeah Milo, and how is she getting on?
>
> *Latvian boy*: Good.
>
> *Inter*: And do you get along well with her? [*Child shakes head*] No? Why not?
>
> *Latvian boy*: Because I don't play with her.
>
> *Inter*: You don't play with her? Yeah, why not?
>
> *Latvian boy*: Because she won't understand anything.
>
> – *P128, Latvian boy, First class, School 5*

> *Local girl*: I think it's kind of weird because you can't understand their accent.
>
> *Inter*: Okay, yeah.
>
> *Local girl*: And when you're trying to talk to them and all they just don't listen to you.
>
> – P53, Local girl, Second class, School 5

In general, most children can be quite sympathetic to the situation of children in their school who have poor English:

> Because when Lena came into our school she had no English at all except yes and no. Like she didn't really understand what we were saying but her brother could speak perfect English and he used to translate everything for the teacher when she came in. And she was very shy and all but I know whenever I go on holidays and I go to a foreign country if someone's talking I hate the way I can't understand them and they keep looking at you and they think you're talking about them and just like so I say it was very, very hard for her coming over here because she had no English at all.
>
> – P30, Local girl, Sixth class, School 6

Sympathy is commonly expressed in terms of a sense of 'it not being their fault' that they do not speak English:

> Sometimes I get on well like with Claudius. Well it is not really his fault because he doesn't really understand English and he doesn't know what we are talking about.
>
> – P150, Local boy, Second class, School 2

> *Inter*: So what do you think of the fact that there are foreign children in your school?

> *Local girl*: Well I don't really mind, it's not their fault where they were born and they're trying their best to speak English and talk.
>
> – P152, Local girl, Fourth class, School 7

However, occasional efforts to reach out to children who do not speak English seem to peter out quite quickly:

> *Local girl 1*: I don't mind, we just try to like make friends but like we try to make friends with Kate but she doesn't talk, like she just stands there like and we knocked for her once and she didn't know what we were saying, so she kind of stood there standing and looking at us so it was kind of difficult.
>
> *Local girl 2*: And we have to ask teacher to ask her, if you want to ask her questions, you have to ask the teacher, cause she wouldn't talk to anybody but the teacher.
>
> – P163/261, Local girls, Second class, School 5

In some cases, there is less sympathy and more annoyance with having to deal with children who do not speak English:

> *Inter*: And what do you think of people in the school who come from different countries?
>
> *Local boy*: Don't like them.
>
> *Inter*: Why?
>
> *Local boy*: Can't understand them.
>
> *Inter*: Anything else? Is there any other reason?
>
> *Local boy*: No.
>
> P176, Local boy, Fourth class, School 1

> *Inter*: Okay, do you guys think that you're the same or different as people from Poland?

Local girl: Different.

Inter: Okay, how do you think that you're different?

Local girl: Because we talk a different language, and I haven't got a clue what they're saying.

– P62, Local girl, Fifth class, School 6

In trying to understand the dynamics of social interaction, it is important to stress that language differences cause problems in the classroom. For the most part, we can say that teachers and schools were unprepared to deal with the sudden influx of different nationalities, and in spite of their best efforts this had an impact which everyone must feel:

> The hardest thing about it is when you have so many different abilities in the class anyway and then you have children coming in half way through the year with no books and no language and you don't really have any idea of where they have come from or what they are like, the parents haven't got English and you are feeling around in the dark really. It is impossible really.
>
> – Teacher 6, Sixth class, School 6

> Well when they come in they haven't got much English and that makes it very hard because they can't actually do the same work that you are doing in the classroom, so you may have to get something that little bit easier for them, you know, they are starting with their letters for their reading whereas obviously in Second class you are a bit bored doing that.
>
> – Teacher 2, Second class, School 2

On the side of the children who are learning English, there can be a period of apprehension as they worry about being able to speak and hear English with confidence. In the following example, what the child appears to be most concerned about is not learning

English as such, but being able to pick up on the idiom and accent of his classmates:

> *Inter*: Okay. And do you ever play with those children that are a bit bad?
>
> *Romanian boy*: No.
>
> *Inter*: Is it hard to get on with them?
>
> *Romanian boy*: I don't understand all the words and I'm afraid I might say something wrong.
>
> – P19, Romanian boy, Fourth class, School 1

Hearing people speak in languages that they do not understand can be a source of irritation for children and even for teachers. On the part of children, irritation and discomfort is usually expressed as a fear that they are being talked about. As one child put it, 'the same as someone whispering when you, are like, beside them'. Such feelings are expressed by English-speaking children in relation to other children speaking languages other than English and by non-English speaking children about hearing English:

> The first time when I came here like I thought that everyone was talking about me, bad stuff or something like that ...
>
> – P266, Polish girl, Sixth class, School 6

In the following extract, a Mongolian child and his local friend both talk about the unease they feel in being in an environment in which people are speaking languages that are not understood:

> *Inter*: So what is it like not being able to speak English then? How does it make you feel not being able to ...
>
> *Mongolian boy*: It is weird. There's all different people around you talking about something that you don't know, what is he saying?

Local boy: It would just be like me going up and they are all talking in his language, I wouldn't know what he is saying.

Inter: And is it hard when you are trying to start speaking, do you ever get afraid that you will say anything wrong or anything like that?

Mongolian boy: Yes, because when you are talking you kind of talk wrong, you miss out on words so that people think you are like a freak or something.

– P168/327, *Local and Mongolian boys, Sixth class, School 1*

These two children then go on to tell an anecdote about a Lithuanian boy in their class. The actual facts behind the story could be interpreted in many ways, but what emerges clearly is the ever present fear that someone talking in a language you do not understand could be saying bad things or talking about you:

Local boy: Because sometimes he'd be talking in his own language and there is another girl in our class and she is from Lithuania and she tells us what he is saying and he doesn't use nice words.

Mongolian boy: And sometimes he curses in his language.

Inter: Sometimes he curses in his language.

Local boy: That is what I mean, he doesn't read or write words, he'd be cursing and that.

Inter: And what do you think of that?

Mongolian boy: Bad.

Local boy: We don't really like it. Sometimes he'd be talking about other people in his own language.

– P168/327, *Local and Mongolian boys, Sixth class, School 1*

We will return to bullying in more depth later, but it is worth pointing out at this stage that it can sometimes be associated with poor English language skills. Children who do not speak English very often experience social isolation because of language barriers. However, migrant children often bear the brunt of more active physical and verbal bullying carried out predominately, though not exclusively, by local children. In the following extract a Polish girl is very clear about the reasons she was physically bullied when she first arrived in her current school:

Polish girl: ... I feel like stupid because of no English I think and always seem like, it was not good for me, and always when I came back home I was crying that they were ...

Inter: Oh no.

Polish girl: ... punching me or something. I was like feeling very bad.

Inter: You were very upset by it, were you? And were these girls in your class?

Polish girl: Yeah.

Inter: Yeah, they were girls in your class, okay. And why do you think they were doing that to you?

Polish girl: Maybe that because I was talking with Karol in Polish and ...

Inter: Okay.

Polish girl: ... I don't know English or something.

Inter: Okay, so you think they were picking on you because you were talking with your cousin as well in Polish?

Polish girl: Yeah. And they maybe thought that I talking about them or something like that.

– P267, *Polish girl, Fifth class, School 7*

While this extract refers to physical bullying, verbal bullying and making fun of children behind their back seem to be more common. In the following extract some local girls laugh about an incident in which a migrant child made a mistake speaking English:

> *Local girl 1*: And she goes 'yeah' like that and then she goes 'did you swim in the swimming pool?' and she said 'no'. [*Laughter*]
>
> *Local girl 2*: And do you swim in puddles and she said 'yeah'. [*Laughter*]
>
> – P 145/229, Local girls, Fourth class, School 7

In the following extract, a young Romanian boy talks about the fears he has of being made fun of when he tries to speak English:

> *Inter*: And is that difficult, like … to talk to someone?
>
> *Romanian boy*: Yeah.
>
> *Inter*: Yeah?
>
> *Romanian boy*: Yeah, and even they could slag ye.
>
> *Inter*: Yeah? What would they be slaggin' ye about?
>
> *Romanian boy*: 'You don't know how to talk English hahahahaha'… and laughin' at ye.
>
> – P136, Romanian boy, Second class, School 2 (*speaking through a translator*)

A variant of this is local children making fun of migrant children when they believe the target child cannot understand them:

> *Inter*: Sometimes they're bad to you, yeah? Would they ever call any of you names or anything like that?
>
> *Slovakian girl*: Yeah, they talking about us or …
>
> *Inter*: Okay.

> *Slovakian girl*: Because they thinking that I don't know English and they thought that I don't understand English and they can talk about me because so how would they feel if they come to my country?
>
> *Inter*: Well, that's it.
>
> *Slovakian girl*: They have to think first about that.
>
> – P317, Slovakian girl, Fifth class, School 7

As mentioned above, bullying related to poor English language skills, when it does occur, is predominately by local children towards children of migrant origin. However, not being able to speak to classmates, or being heavily dependant on others to do so, can produce power differentials which can be easily exploited by anybody.

> *Inter*: What about you, Naomi, you said yes, that they treat you differently because you're from a different country?
>
> *Filipino girl*: Yeah, they treat me a little not-nice, like this one girl from another country didn't understand exactly what I say.
>
> *Inter*: Okay, is that somebody from Ireland or somebody from another country?
>
> *Filipino girl*: Somebody from another country.
>
> – P87, Filipino girl, Fourth class, School 3

In the following extract, we get a third party perspective, a local and a Mongolian child talking about how they do not like the fact that a Romanian child in their class bullies another Romanian child who does not speak English:

> *Local child*: He usually picks on Anton.
>
> *Inter*: He picks on Anton, and Anton is new as well. And why do you think he picks on Anton?

> *Mongolian child*: Because he is afraid to go to us.
>
> *Local child*: He is afraid to hit anybody else or bully anybody else so he bullies Anton because he knows Anton is weak because he doesn't know much English.
>
> – P168/327, Local and Mongolian boys, Sixth class, School 1

But, of course, migrant children make progress and may acquire local slang and accents. Here a local girl reviews the language abilities of the foreign nationals who live on the same road as she does:

> Vanessa she went back to Hungary and she is kind of learning our accent and Alice and Camilla, Camilla just needs to learn a bit more and Alice knows loads and her Mam and Dad need to learn a bit more as well. They don't know like anything what we say to the kids or anything like that.
>
> – P53, Local girl, Second class, School 5

By comparison, children of migrant parents who have been here for a long time seem to fare much better:

> *Local girl 1*: But Anna is just like completely English.
>
> *Inter*: Yeah, she wasn't.
>
> *Local girl 2*: She's been in it like since she was like a baby, this school, so …
>
> *Local girl 1*: Yeah.
>
> *Local girl 2*: … she gets on.
>
> – P308/235, Local girls, Fifth class, School 7

Settling In

Most migrant children report that, at a certain point, they had acquired the language and after that things became easier and they started to settle in:

> *Filipino girl*: It was just like that I had nobody to talk with, just stay in the bench eating and watching the people running around.
>
> *Inter*: Okay, and what happened then, has that changed, it's not the same because I see you running around now.
>
> *Filipino girl*: Yeah ...
>
> – P87, *Filipino girl, Fourth class, School 6*

> *Inter*: Do you think you are the same or different from people from Ireland?
>
> *Nigerian boy*: The same, well I used to be different but now I am kind of the same.
>
> – P271, *Nigerian boy, Second class, School 4*

Local children are also well aware of this phenomenon:

> *Local girl 1*: Yeah like the people that do move over from like foreign countries and all they like they kind of get used to living in [*the local area*] after a while and then like they like start like learning how to speak English and they do like so it's ...
>
> *Inter*: So they're kind of like the same yeah okay.
>
> *Local girl 2*: It would be hard for them and all but like they pick up so real quick.
>
> – P31/59, *Local girls, Sixth class, School 6*

The process of learning English not only facilitates communication between local and migrant children but also between different groups of migrant children:

> *Russian girl*: I had a little friend from Africa, she moved though, and when we first met it was kind of hard because she didn't really know any English.
>
> *Inter*: Okay.
>
> *Russian girl*: And it was hard for me to understand what she was trying to tell me or something ...
>
> *Inter*: Okay.
>
> *Russian girl*: ... because she didn't know much but like then she knew a lot more.
>
> – P322, Russian girl, Fifth class, School 7

However, this process of learning English and adjusting to the local situation can have the effect of distancing the child from their native language and culture somewhat:

> *Inter*: Okay. And if you went back to Poland do you think you would become more Polish again?
>
> *Polish girl*: No.
>
> *Inter*: No?
>
> *Polish girl*: ... sometimes when – I was in Poland just like – I don't know when we actually went – but, you know, I went to the shop and I was speaking English and then just because I forgot I was in like Poland ...
>
> *Inter*: Yeah?
>
> *Polish girl*: ... just like the cashier was just looking at me and then I said 'sorry' in Polish and I started to talk Polish.
>
> – P266, Polish girl, Sixth class, School 6

Educational Experience

When this research took place (2008), many children in Dublin from a migrant background would only have had experience with the Irish educational system and with the school they were attending at the time. They were born in Ireland or had moved here before they were of school going age.

However, talking to older children who migrated to Ireland and who can remember their previous experiences in school two things clearly emerge. Firstly, many recall a school experience in their country of origin that was 'harder': it involved a more advanced curriculum, a longer school day, more homework and tougher discipline. Secondly, as might be expected, for many of these children their school lives has been marked by great disruption and upheaval. Both of these facts can create challenges for the children involved, and can increase the distance between them and their local peers.

The 'hardness' of school seems to be a feature of migrant children's experiences across different countries of origin, but it is particularly striking in accounts by children from Eastern Europe. Here children from three different countries talk about their experiences of education before coming to Ireland:

> *Romanian girl*: When we have summer holidays they give you a book like to read all that and all the chapters to describe and for maths it is like a book, all the pages.

> *Lithuanian girl*: In Lithuania in the summer you have to do ... in first class you have to read three books and in the fourth class you have to read about eight or nine, not like tiny ones like that.

> *Inter*: And is there a big difference between Poland and here?

> *Polish girl*: Yes, from fourth class you start spelling tests, big tests and in Ireland you start work in first class but in second class you are playing. In Poland in first class you have to study how to write properly.

— P23/108/196, Lithuanian, Polish and Romanian girls, Sixth class, School 1

The curriculum which these children are used to has often been very challenging, particularly in the areas of mathematics, spelling and history. Here Polish and Slovakian girls talk about why their previous schools were harder:

Polish girl: And we have to know like maths and Polish language, that's a very hard language …

Inter: Okay.

Polish girl: … and history about Poland and things.

Inter: Okay, you seem to do a lot. And what's the difference between your school in Slovakia and this school here? Is there much difference?

Both children: Yeah.

Inter: Yeah? What sort of differences are there?

Slovakian girl: The mathematics.

Inter: Okay, yeah.

Slovakian girl: The spellings.

— P267/317/340, Two Slovakian girls and one Polish girl, Fifth class, School 7

This more 'fact-based' curriculum is complemented by more homework and a longer school day:

No, in my country there was lots of homework.

— P74, Mauritian girl, Fourth class, School 6

One of the schools, the earliest school that I ever started, it started at 7:30.

— P16, Nigerian boy, Sixth class, School 2

> You have to go in the school 7:30 until 5:00.
>
> – P5, Nigerian girl, Fourth class, School 3

Migrant children sometimes also report that they are used to the one-teacher, one-subject system which is a feature of Irish secondary schools but which is very different from the close relation-ship with a single class teacher which is the system in Irish primary schools:

> We get different teacher for one subject but in every day we get same teacher but in one subject.
>
> – P26, Filipino girl, Fourth class, School 3

> Yes like the work is different. Like even in the primary school there are loads of teachers teaching different subjects, it is not the same teacher.
>
> – P16, Nigerian boy, Sixth class, School 2

Occasionally, children report experiences with education systems that seem more variable:

> On Monday a teacher teach us, on Tuesdays another teacher.
>
> – P5, Nigerian girl, Fourth class, School 3

There is also a sense of a different style of teaching which complements the emphasis on facts. Here, for example, a Georgian boy talks about learning by rote:

> Like they give us about poems up to here and all we have to learn those stories off by heart.
>
> – P240, Georgian boy, Second class, School 1

There are also further indications that the style of teaching which these students are familiar with is more traditional and authoritarian than that which they experience in Ireland:

> This one [school] is quite different because in Latvia the teachers scream sometimes, like they don't like something and like my brother doesn't like school in Latvia because everybody screaming ...
>
> – P124, Latvian girl, Fourth class, School 3

> Yes, but when you get late from school they smack you. And on Friday if you have no hair up like a pony tail they ask you to cut it off.
>
> – P5, Nigerian girl, Fourth class, School 3

Migrant children often report that they are happier with the physical conditions of their school in Ireland:

> *Mauritian girl*: Because in my country there's no Library.
>
> *Inter*: Okay. You like the Library here?
>
> *Mauritian girl*: Yeah.
>
> – P74, Mauritian girl, Fourth class, School 6

> *Inter*: And in Latvia were there more students in the classroom?
>
> *Latvian girl*: Yeah, it's very big classes and I think so 100.
>
> – P124, Latvian girl, Fourth class, School 3

For many of these children, their school life has been marked by repeated changes of school, both in Ireland and in other countries. In some of the most extreme cases, children reported having attended as many as 12, 13 and 14 schools prior to the one that they were in when interviewed. Inevitably, such repeated changes are stressful:

> It is hard you have to make new friends, new friends, new friends.
>
> – P26, Nigerian girl, Fourth class, School 3

> It's a big change though coming in like the middle – like everybody is finishing up here and that kind of thing in a way.
>
> – P266, Polish girl, Sixth class, School 6

Already some of these children are not looking forward to having to move again:

> *Latvian girl*: I will go to America because my dad says it has like English too and we will come back in here and I wish I will come back in here and my mom say that we will be able to finish this school and I will be happy.
>
> *Inter*: You will be happy about that – you don't want to go to America?
>
> *Latvian girl*: No, because like it's different and I know Ireland, not America, because I don't know what's in America.
>
> – P124, Latvian girl, Fourth class, School 3

Although it can hardly be classed as an advantage it is sometimes possible to detect a certain 'toughness' that has grown up in response to these constant changes:

> *Inter*: How many [schools]?
>
> *Polish girl*: I don't know, four.
>
> *Inter*: Four, wow.
>
> *Polish girl*: Yeah, it's not many but it's like very hard sometimes when I got into a new school ...
>
> *Inter*: Yeah.
>
> *Polish girl*: ... 'cause I don't know any kids and that kind of stuff and when they're talking and when they're looking I think that they're laughing about – like at me or something ...

Inter: Yeah.

Polish girl: ... but then I don't care.

– P266, Polish girl, Sixth class, School 6

Approach to School and Educational Performance

This research did not aim to examine academic outlook or performance and these are areas that children of this age will rarely choose to talk about. However, from occasional comments, our own observations and teacher interviews, it emerged clearly that, in general, these migrant children approach school with a very positive attitude. There was also anecdotal evidence suggesting that in these schools some migrant children may outperform local children academically.

> *Teacher 1*: When you are talking about children who come in who have the language, there are an awful lot of children who are just streets ahead, they are just flying along and it is great because the rest of the class then, they'd be a bit competitive and if they see this guy finishing early all the time they are saying, we need to speed up to be as good as him. So there are an awful lot of children –
>
> *Teacher 2*: A lot of the Eastern Europeans, like their standard is much higher than here.
>
> *Teacher 1*: And they have gorgeous writing and everything.
>
> *Teacher 2*: And their maths is very good and tables.
>
> – Teachers 1 and 2, Second class, School 2

Particularly this year, I find its just a pleasure to give out a rhyme for them to practice at home, or two pages of reading ... they come back and they've four or five pages of reading done ... they have been an asset without a doubt ... It certainly has raised our results in standardised tests.

– *Teacher 6, Senior Infants Class, School 7*

They [newcomers] are very bright, brighter than a lot of kids here.

– *Teacher 5, Sixth class, School 6*

The following account by a teacher gives us an archetypical image of a hard-working migrant pupil:

She [Justine] is extremely hard working, extremely conscientious, she is well able to stand on her own two feet, she won't actually allow others to talk her out of doing something, you know, she is very focused and she is a nice girl as well. She takes time to help others ...

– *Teacher 5, Fifth class, School 6*

A local girl in the same class comments on the same child:

Justine is always finished first but it's like everybody is having a race to be first.

– *P56, Local girl, Fifth class, School 6*

In general, it appears that these migrant children come to school with a different outlook on education and school than their local peers. Here, for example, a Latvian girl talks about what makes her happy in school:

Playing games. Doing the maths.

– *P124, Latvian girl, Fourth class, School 3*

By contrast, here two local children talk about how much they hate maths:

Local girl 1: I hate maths and Irish.

Local girl 2: Maths 'cause you do it 24/7.

Local girl 1: We're doing it now in there.

Inter: Oh are you?

Local girl 1: And now we've stopped.

Local girl 1: We're here having a good time.

Local girl 2: So we're happy here, missing out on maths time.

– P234/308, Local girls, Fifth class, School 7

The difference seems to extend to many subject areas. Here, for example, a Polish and a local child talk about learning Irish:

Inter: And what about you Michael, do you speak any other languages?

Local boy: No.

Inter: Do you speak Irish?

Local boy: No.

Inter: Do you like Irish class?

Local boy: No.

Polish boy: I do.

Inter: And what do you like about it?

Polish boy: I like it because there are nice teachers.

Inter: And what about you, why do you not like Irish?

Local boy: Because I hate this school.

– P96/294, Polish and Local boy, Second class, School 1

These differences in outlook do create social tensions. Here, for example, a Mauritian child talks about the fact that other children chat during lessons. This annoys her, yet she says nothing for fear of being thought 'bad' by the other children:

> *Filipino girl*: Sometimes you just don't understand subjects because we don't understand English very much and there are people talking and we just can't hear what people is saying.
>
> *Inter*: Okay, so if there are people talking you find it hard to focus.
>
> *Mauritian girl*: Yeah they just talk, not even about school, they talk about high school musical …
>
> *Inter*: During the class?
>
> *Mauritian girl*: Yeah, but I can't say nothing they would think that I'm bad.
>
> – *P87/112, Filipino and Mauritian girls, Fourth class, School 3*

As always, however, it is worth pointing out that we are writing in general terms and there are many exceptions. Here, for example, is an Irish girl talking about what makes her happy in school:

> *Local girl*: Just say like when you've been good in class all week and you get person of the week or something like that.
>
> *Inter*: Oh yeah and do you often get person of the week?
>
> *Local girl*: Yeah, sometimes, I got it last week.
>
> – *P218, Local girl, Sixth class, School 6*

Teachers, in general, seem to agree that migrant children have raised the overall academic standards of their schools. However, there is some disagreement on the extent to which migrant pupils have had a positive impact on the performance of the local children in terms of a general raising of standards. Here, for example, a fourth year teacher talks about how the standards have been raised in her class:

> *Teacher*: Yeah and I mean by and large the children that have arrived from abroad have been very diligent, very hard working, good work ethic and an appreciation for education so they, you know, they have raised the standard in some aspects, like in terms of studying and focusing on work, so it is a nice development too.
>
> *Inter*: And do you think that has an impact on the other students?
>
> *Teacher*: Well, I think it motivates, any good student in the class will motivate the others to do better and I think it does add to the work ethic in the classroom, that, you know, education is important.
>
> –*Teacher 3, Fourth class, School 3*

On the other hand, here a Senior Infants teacher is more cautious about the effect:

> It makes my job a lot easier if twelve of them are going to come in with their homework done and maybe a couple of pages extra done ... whether it rubs off or not, I couldn't say yet, its kind of ... too early.
>
> – *Teacher 6, Senior Infants class, School 7*

Although our research was not specifically looking at issues to do with academic performance, our class time observations would tend to suggest that both of these views may be correct. Sometimes there does appear to be a general raising of standards and sometimes not.

However, academic prowess is not always held in high regard in children's social worlds. These differences in attitudes towards education, therefore, inevitably have ramifications for social relations between migrant and local children over and above the potentially positive influence of more diligent students on their classmates. Here, a teacher talks about her impressions of this:

> The international children have more support at home and generally get on better in school and sometimes this can lead them to be seen as 'goody-goodies'.
>
> –Teacher 7, Second class, School 4

Family and Out of School Hours

Differences in academic outlook and performance are often related to differences in family ethos and how time is spent outside of school hours. Migrant children often mention the high aspirations that their parents have for them.

> Oh my Da ... want me to be – do you know those people that they – they're on the TV and they showed the money ... like the money increases or it decreases, the amount of money in China.
>
> – P122, Romanian boy, Sixth class, School 1

Migrant children also seem to be familiar with a very well ordered family life:

> First I go home and get on my clothes and then I wash my hands, I go to play and my mommy says you go and play while I'm making the food. When the food is ready, I go and eat. Then I ask my sister if she can play with me and I play. Sometimes I draw.
>
> – P165, Romanian girl, Senior Infants class, School 7

Talking to local and migrant children about how they spend time outside of school a typical pattern emerges: migrant children spend more time at home, engage in fewer formal activities, socialise less with same age peers and generally have more responsibilities at home. A number of migrant children refer to chores that they have to do at home, the two most typical being cleaning and child minding. In the following extract, a Mongolian and a local boy discuss what they will be doing at the weekend:

> *Local boy*: Probably go and stay in my cousins, I do go out to them every week ... every weekend because I don't really see them, they live far out. So I go out and stay either Friday or Saturday every week.
>
> *Inter*: What about you, what do you usually do at the weekend?
>
> *Mongolian boy*: Usually I have to mind my sister all day.
>
> *Inter*: What age is she?
>
> *Mongolian boy*: She is going to be two on the [date removed].
>
> *Inter*: That is an awful lot of work.
>
> *Mongolian boy*: All day, Saturday and Sunday. Well not this week because my ma is staying home.
>
> *Inter*: What do you think about minding your sister?
>
> *Mongolian boy*: It is fun.
>
> – P168/327, *Local and Mongolian boys, Sixth class, School 1*

The doing of chores appears to occur across national groups and to begin quite young by Irish standards. Here, for example, a young Indian and a young Romanian girl, both in Senior Infants, talk proudly of the chores they do at home:

> *Indian girl*: I would help my mam.
>
> *Romanian girl*: I help my mam too.
>
> *Inter*: You help your mam too Paula?
>
> *Romanian girl*: And the granny, and my granny said can I help her.

Inter: You help her?

Indian girl: And I clean out the room for my mammy.

– P172/265, Romanian and Indian girls, Senior Infants class, School 7

As we might expect, some children were far less enthusiastic about having to do chores at home:

Inter: And do you ever play, when you're not at school, then do you ever play with younger kids? [*Shakes head*] No? Why wouldn't you play with younger kids?

Nigerian boy: Because we have to – me and my brother have to do all the work in the house.

Inter: Oh do you, right. So what kind of work do you do?

Nigerian boy: We have to sweep the floor, wash the dishes and sometimes we go to bed at six o'clock.

Inter: Okay right, so you do a lot of work. And do you like doing that or …? [*Childs nods no.*] No you don't like it?

Nigerian boy: We don't get time to do anything.

Inter: You don't have time to do anything. And what would you like to do instead of all the chores?

Nigerian boy: Watching TV, playing my PlayStation …

Inter: Yeah.

Nigerian boy: … and going outside.

– P268, Nigerian boy, Second class, School 2

Interestingly, this particular child looks forward to going back to Nigeria because, when there, he is freed from having to do chores.

Nigerian boy: I get to relax in Nigeria because I don't do all the work.

> *Inter*: You don't do all the work, oh. Are there other people to do the work in Nigeria? Yeah.
>
> *Nigerian boy*: My uncles.
>
> – P268, Nigerian boy, Second class, School 2

Other children look forward to the day when some other member of the family will take responsibility for their chores, usually a younger sibling or an elderly relative. Here, Nigerian and Filipino girls, both of whom appear to have quite substantial home duties, discuss their possibilities:

> *Inter*: Okay, you have to do a lot of those household chores do you?
>
> *Filipino girl*: My nails got white, like playing with water in the swimming pool.
>
> *Nigerian girl*: When my grandma isn't there I have to wash the dishes, clean the house and do the chores. But when she is coming here, I don't do it anymore.
>
> *Filipino girl*: I don't like the way my life has been because I have to wash the dishes, do everything.
>
> *Inter*: You have to do a lot of chores do you?
>
> *Filipino girl*: Yes, every night when we eat like when it is twelve o'clock my mum says I have to wash the dishes before I go to bed. And sometimes I sneak into the bedroom and sleep and I wake up early to wash the dishes.
>
> *Inter*: That is hard.
>
> *Filipino girl*: I wish I were number four.
>
> *Inter*: Because you are the eldest is it?
>
> *Filipino girl*: Yes still when my sister grows up and gets married, I will still be the one washing the dishes.
>
> *Inter*: Really?

Filipino girl: Yes.

Inter: Are you the eldest?

Filipino girl: Yes.

Inter: That is the way it is, that is the tradition is it?

Filipino girl: So when my sister is ten now, she is the one that is going to be washing the dishes.

—P5/26, Nigerian and Filipino girls, Fourth class, School 3

In general, local children seem to have far more playtime, both unsupervised and organised. There are, of course, exceptions and some local children are heavily committed to the care of younger siblings and elderly relatives.

With a few notable exceptions, the vast majority of migrant children spend their out of school leisure hours in a typical way: at home, engaged in sedentary activities, playing alone or with siblings. This pattern is more pronounced among girls. Here are some characteristic answers to the question 'What do you do when you are not at school?':

Mauritian girl: Watch TV and I go to the library, sometimes I with my mom brought me shopping.

Inter: What about you Michelle?

Filipino girl: I go to the … sometimes go to the mall with my mom …

Inter: To the which?

Filipino girl: Go to the mall with my mom and watch TV and sometimes coming to my aunt's house.

— P 87/112, Mauritian and Filipino girls, Fourth class, School 3

Romanian girl: I go home and some people come and visit me.

Local girl: ... mostly she sits in and watches the Disney Channel.

–P222/291, *Romanian and Irish girls, Fourth class, School 1*

The computer.

– P69, *Romanian girl, Senior Infants class, School 7*

I like to paint some things for my ma.

– P219, *Kosovar girl, Senior Infants class, School 7*

Another common playtime activity for girls outside of school is playing with younger siblings:

Pakistani girl: I play with my small brother.

Inter: The four month old?

Pakistani girl: Yeah.

– P241, *Pakistani girl, Sixth class, School 3*

Play with my little brother.

– P26, *Nigerian girl, Fourth class, School 3*

Kosovar girl: I play with my brother.

Inter: Oh wow, how old is he?

Kosovar girl: Four.

– P219, *Kosovar girl, Senior Infants class, School 7*

Watching TV and using the computer are also frequently mentioned by the boys as well, although periods of outdoor sport relieve the general pattern of what still is a very structured and home-based social world. Again, the question is 'What do you do when you are not at school?':

Georgian boy: Just play.

Inter: Yeah.

Georgian boy: Play football.

Inter: Yeah?

Georgian boy: Watch TV.

Romanian boy: And sometimes I ...

Georgian boy: Go on the laptop.

Romanian boy: ... and sometimes he has, he has a laptop and we watch movies like.

Inter: Okay cool.

Romanian boy: Like all the new movies.

— *P240/122, Georgian and Romanian boys, Sixth class, School 1*

I go to Phoenix Park to play football or something then I go with bicycles and then home on the computer and do my homework.

— *P278, Lithuanian boy, Sixth class, School 4*

When I go to school, when I go home I have an hour to play, but now my father is at home, I have less free time and I start work more on the homework.

— *P19, Romanian boy, Fourth class, School 1*

Migrant children appear to access a far more limited range of organised activities outside of school than their local counterparts. The most common organised activities mentioned by migrant children were those associated with churches, homework and book clubs. There does seem to be a motivation on the part of at least some migrant children to be involved in other activities locally:

Lithuanian girl: Sometimes I am going to the library.

Inter: And if there was a place near you that had more like international kids, would you go then?

Lithuanian girl: Yes.

– P23, Lithuanian girl, Sixth class, School 1

No here I don't play with anyone, I just go to the clubs because my dad will want me to be adapted to the country here. I just go to clubs in the school.

– P87, Filipino girl, Fourth class, School 3

However, a number of children report attempts to become involved in locally organised activities that did not work out very well. This can vary from experiencing a sense of unease to feelings of threat in the activity setting:

Inter: Okay, and tell me then, are you in any groups outside school, clubs or groups or anything. You are in that football club?

Mongolian boy: That was a while ago but it is gone now. The team got back together but the team is now full of bullies.

– P327, Mongolian boy, Sixth class, School 1

Inter: And are any of you in any clubs or groups when you are not in school like?

Polish girl: There is a group beside my house but I am not going there because there is all Irish people and I don't feel comfortable.

– P108, Polish girl, Sixth class, School 1

Revealingly, in one case a migrant child who is currently attending a local basketball club mentions that her only friend in the club is another migrant child:

> *Inter*: And have you made friends at the club then?
>
> *Mauritian girl*: No, Blessing goes to that club, she is from Nigeria, she is my friend in basketball club.
>
> – P112, Mauritian girl, Fourth class, School 3

In a small number of cases, more successful engagement with locally organised activities is possible but almost exclusively for boys engaged with local sports teams.

As a final comment on the issue of migrant children and engagement with organised activities, the following exchange neatly summarises the basic realities of many children's lives and gives a clear indication of the value of follow-up questions:

> *Inter*: And are you in any clubs or groups or anything like that, or teams? [*Child nods.*] Yes, you are in a club are you, what club is that?
>
> *Romanian girl*: Friends and a clubhouse.
>
> *Inter*: That is great, where is your clubhouse?
>
> *Romanian girl*: At the back of my garden.
>
> – P69, Romanian girl, Senior Infants class, School 7

As well as sports, teams, churches and Saturday or weekend schools, the highlight of the weekend for many children is a 'trip' with their parents to a local site or to a relative. Again, this demonstrates that there is very little contact between local and migrant children outside of the school hours.

Reinforcing this point is another feature of the social life of a small number of these children outside of school hours. Some of these children are part of friendship groups with children from the same country of origin as themselves. These groups are not school-based. They are sometimes based in an area, but more commonly build upon family or parental friendship networks.

Inter: Okay, do you have any other friends then, do you ever meet friends from Latvia?

Latvian girl: Yeah, Pearl.

Inter: Okay, and how do you know her?

Latvian girl: Him.

Inter: Him, or sorry how do you know him?

Latvian girl: He knows my mom and we went speaking Latvian and then together we know him, together we are friends now.

– P124, Latvian girl, Fourth class, School 3

Inter: So are you part of any clubs or groups or anything when you're not in school?

Polish girl: Like where I live, like after school at my house, I live beside Karol so we can talk together …

Inter: Okay.

Polish girl: … and we got another two friends from Poland …

Inter: Okay.

Polish girl: … so we can play with them and talk to them.

– P267, Polish girl, Fifth class, School 7

Another Polish girl described one of these networks which is unusual in that it appears to be quite large and includes boys and girls of very different ages:

Inter: Outside school do you have any friends who are boys?

Polish girl: Yeah, there's a few boys I know and like I hang around with them.

Inter: Okay.

Polish girl: Yeah, I have – like I know older boys say about eighteen.

Inter: Eighteen yeah?

Polish girl: And sixteen yeah.

Inter: Okay.

Polish girl: They very nice.

Inter: Are they?

Polish girl: Yeah, they always minding me like so I can go out with them and I can come like back like very – at night, because my Ma knows them.

Inter: Okay, alright. And they are your friends, are they?

Polish girl: Yeah one boy I can go with like outside all the time to be like very like – he lives just beside me.

Inter: Yeah.

Polish girl: Yeah. So that's why my Ma lets.

Inter: Okay. Is he from Poland as well?

Polish girl: Yeah.

Inter: Okay so you're Mam knows him.

Polish girl: My Ma knows his Ma so that's why I can go.

– P266, Polish girl, Sixth class, School 6

Not all young migrants have such networks however:

Inter: So what about in your area, do you feel the same or different from people in your area?

Nigerian boy: A bit different.

Inter: In what way do you feel a bit different? Just in your area where you live?

Nigerian boy: Because there are not lots of people that like me so that is why I try and make friends.

Inter: Okay, so how do you feel about that?

Nigerian boy: I feel a bit sad.

– P339, *Nigerian boy, Second class, School 2*

The Experience of Migration

The experience of migration can in itself help to create some distance between local and newcomer children. Although this is something which migrant children are unlikely to notice themselves, the interviews indicate that they often have a breadth of perspective from being immersed in more than one culture. Even the more challenging aspects of moving from one country to another can involve learning. Many have also enjoyed exposure to different languages from an early age, and it is quite common to meet children who can speak two or three languages. This facility with language can often help to create the unexpected situation in which migrant children can often outperform local children in Gaeilge.

Discussion

Allowing for exceptions, the migrant children we encountered in this research were industrious, well-behaved and had a positive attitude towards school. Both they and their teachers report that their families supported them strongly in their educational ambitions. This general picture is reflected in the results of other studies and, by now, a typical picture has emerged of migrants living in Ireland as being well-educated and highly motivated. Barrett, Bergin and Duffy (2006), using an analysis of the Household Quarterly Survey, found that immigrants in Ireland were a highly educated group, although they were not always employed in occupations that fully reflect their education levels. A more recent analysis by Barrett and Kelly (2008) using more complete Census data argues that earlier conclusions drawn from the Household Quarterly Survey are generally accurate. Fanning et al. (2011) found that immigrants in the South Dublin 'Liberties' were far more likely to have third-level education than their local counterparts and were more likely to be in full-time employment. These survey results only relate to adults. However, existing research also confirms the impression of the children of migrants as being highly motivated and well-disposed towards school. Teachers in the study by Devine and Kelly (2002) noted an impressive work ethic and respect for authority in such children, while Devine (2009) discusses the ways in which migrant children seek to maximise the exchange value of their education. Focus groups with teachers in Dublin 15 found that migrant pupils were rated as doing well academically (in areas in which English was not a requirement) and as having very high levels of motivation (McGorman and Sugrue, 2007). A national survey of school principals also found that 'newcomer students' tended to rate quite well on academic achievement and very highly on motivation in relation to their school work (Smith, Darmody, McGinnity and Byrne, 2009). Fanning et al. (2011) found that, compared to local children in the 'Liberties', migrant children had fewer problems in and out of school and had parents with more optimistic views about their educational prospects. One final incidental observation is worth mentioning. Both this study and the study by Devine and Kelly (2002) found that some teachers, who were initially wary of teaching in multi-cultural schools, became far more positive over time. Overall, migrant children appear to approach education with a very positive attitude and many do quite well.

This may of course change, even in the very near future. Firstly, given the economic downturn, we could argue that the migrants most likely to leave are those with the greatest social resources. On the other hand, as the recession is global, migrants have not been leaving in large numbers (CSO, 2009) and we might reasonably expect that families are less likely to move at short notice than singletons. On the basis of our experience, we would argue that, if there is a 'drain' on the migrant population such that the better educated and more capable move on, that this may affect the level of academic ability among migrant children but not the positive attitude to school and education which appears to be quite consistent.

There may also be concerns about what will happen over time as migrant children settle in. In 1993, Portes and Zhou argued that, in unequal societies, integration does not automatically result in upwards social mobility. Rather, they contend that the outcome of the process is heavily influenced by which segment of society particular immigrant groups integrate into (see also Portes and Rumbaut, 2001). As we have noted earlier, Dublin's north inner-city is an area long associated with deprivation and educational disadvantage. Although some possible raising of standards in inner-city schools has been suggested in our findings, Portes and Zhou's argument means that we may also expect the effect to work in the opposite direction: a gradual hemorrhaging of positive attitudes and work ethic among migrant children the longer time they spend in Ireland. On the other hand, however, Kasintz et al. (2008) argue that the ability to draw on two different cultures when negotiating challenges or making everyday decisions is a distinct advantage for migrant children. It remains to be seen whether or not the migrant children that are the focus of our study are able to use these advantages to avoid obstacles such as discrimination and blocked aspirations traditionally faced by minority groups.

Our research shows that children of migrant children living in Dublin's north inner-city have positive attitudes towards school, often do comparatively well academically and tend to come from families with traditional values emphasising the importance of education, respect for authority and responsibility to the family. As a result of this and other factors, we find that they are often different in many ways from their local peers. The issue is to understand the implications of these differences. The first, more obvious point is that this academic ambition is not yet general knowledge. Public ideas about migrant young people have been, to a large extent, influenced by the experiences of other countries such as England, France and the US. From the point of view of social values among children and young people, the Irish story of immigration to date is largely a positive one. The second point is crucial to the present research: how do positive education values of immigrants affect social interaction with local peers in the kinds of school which the majority of migrant children will attend? The present research clearly shows that different attitudes to school can add to social distance between migrant and local children, even in situations in which there is initial warmth. The implications are important when we come to think about intervention as we should have a full understanding of the barriers before we attempt to remove them. Theorising and approaches to intervention are often based on a model of simple cultural difference. The situation seems in fact to be more complicated and more challenging. In the final analysis, a certain amount of value conflict is perhaps inevitable. However, children are adaptable and, if the situation is handled properly, they may be able to learn much from one another and benefit greatly from the experience of both cultural and social diversity.

Family practices also seem to have a large impact on social interaction outside of school hours. This again poses a major challenge for the future of integration in the inner-city. In this and in other studies, it has been found that, by and large, school is the only site in which local and migrant children regularly interact. Outside of school hours, migrant children are mostly at home, often engaged in household duties. In general, they seem to partake of both formal and informal leisure activities far less than their local peers. In Devine and Kelly's study (2002), teachers expressed concern about lack of integration outside of school hours, and a shortage of after-school activities was also noted as a barrier to integration in the Dublin 15 study (McGorman and Sugrue, 2007).

Chapter 5

Social Interaction 1: Learning Together

In this chapter, we discuss different categories of positive social interaction that occur between migrant and local children, including: reaching out, opportunities at yard time and a general sense that multi-culturalism is the new norm. It is argued that important positive influences on inter-ethnic relations exist, but that there are also clear limits to how these translate into reality.

Good inter-community relations can be said to be marked by feelings of tolerance, respect, warmth, generosity, openness and engagement. When difficulties occur, they may be highly visible. This can make it easy to overlook the fact that smooth and harmonious inter-community relations may often be the norm, woven unobtrusively and seamlessly into the fabric of children's social worlds.

It is important to document these positive features for a number of reasons:

- To produce a complete picture of the situation as the basis for future action. Partial pictures tend to produce partial and easily misdirected solutions. The classic example of this is the multi-cultural education programme which appears to work because it converts the converted a little more, yet risks leaving the 'resistant' as deeply entrenched as ever (if not more so).

- Detailed examination of how things work well help us to understand better what we may be doing right, what we need to keep doing and may also point towards how to improve more problematic situations.

Not all migrant children are socially excluded. Some may have very extensive social networks, benefiting from connections with local children and connections made through family and community networks. The following is an unusual case of a Polish girl in sixth class who complains that she has so many friends:

> *Polish girl*: Yeah, I have a lot of friends so, sometimes when someone is walking and say 'hi' to me I don't know who is it but I remember that I know that person.
>
> *Inter*: Yeah?
>
> *Polish girl*: ... yeah, so it's very hard.
>
> – P266, Polish girl, Sixth class, School 6

This is an atypical example and may represent the extreme end of a spectrum of social connectedness. It is worth noting that the girl in question is acculturated to an extent that she can 'pass herself off' as a local girl when she wishes.

In this chapter, we will examine a number of phenomena which are perhaps less striking but nonetheless reveal positive experiences of inter-community relations. We will be looking at the following themes:

- Reaching out
- Willing to get along ... positive but qualified
- The new norm
- Opportunities at yard time
- Closer friendships.

Reaching Out

A phenomenon which often appears in our data is that of local children 'reaching out' to migrant children, a typical scenario being a migrant child who is relatively new to the school and quite isolated being invited to join a game or being offered some assistance by a local child. The following are two typical examples related by local children:

> *Local girl*: And like when Katie is out in the yard she doesn't have anyone to play with but me and Niamh always ask her to play, don't we?
>
> – P71/250, Local girl, Sixth class, School 5

> *Local girl 1*: There was a girl in our class last year …
>
> *Local girl 2*: Called Ana.
>
> *Local girl 1*: … who couldn't speak any English at all …
>
> Inter: Yeah?
>
> *Local girl 1*: … but we'd go over to her and she'd be drawing and we'd say 'that's a lovely drawing' and she'd started laughing and all.
>
> *Local girl 2*: Her name is Ana and she's from Romania.
>
> *Local girl 1*: She was a gorgeous drawer. She could draw these lovely dresses.
>
> – P55/305, Local girls, Fourth class, School 6

But this willingness to engage may not always endure. In the following example, we also see the way in which children who engage in reaching out may lose interest and fail to follow up on efforts to help:

> *Local girl*: Yeah, and you know what and I thought this is a good thing when we play Golden time like she had no one to play with right and I, I was just, she was just standing there like and I, I could see in her face, she was saying would someone come over and like play with me and I come over and asked her did she want to play Ma's with me and then she was happy then.

> *Inter*: Yeah that's nice, 'cause sometimes I do see her playing, I see her on her own, or she doesn't talk that much, she doesn't seem to have that many friends ...
>
> – *P297, Local girl, Fourth class, School 6*

In a later section, we will discuss circumstances when such attempts to reach out do not work out too well, when they are perceived as tokenistic or are misunderstood. For example, in the final case above we may detect from the interviewer's comments that the reaching out was never followed-up and the migrant child remains quite isolated. However, it is important to note that for newly arrived or excluded children, incidents of reaching out can be important events. Even when they do not lead on to continuing, close relationships, migrant children can speak warmly of local children who have helped them at one time or another. A girl who is quite ostracised and occasionally bullied speaks fondly of a girl in her class who occasionally helps her:

> I like Jane. Sometimes she helps me, she's good for me.
>
> – *P241, Pakistani girl, Fifth class, School 3*

Classes can vary quite substantially in terms of both the positive and negative things which occur. The picture in each classroom and class group may be quite fluid and complex. We will return to this key point in Chapter 8. Here we can note that in some cases, migrant children report feeling very welcome when they arrive into their class. Important in the following extract is the fact that the child being interviewed goes on to talk about the actual moments when she was helped:

> *Inter*: And what do you think of the other girls in your class in general?
>
> *Nigerian girl*: Nice, they are kind and helpful.
>
> *Inter*: In what way are they kind?

> *Nigerian girl*: They were helping, like when I was sad they make me happy.
>
> *Inter*: Okay, they cheer you up. And when you started in school first did they help you?
>
> *Nigerian girl*: I didn't have any lunch and Katie gave me lunch.
>
> *Inter*: That was good, wasn't it?
>
> *Nigerian girl*: And Kelly gave me a sandwich.
>
> – P5, *Nigerian girl, Fourth class, School 3*

This kind of reaching out may be repeated over a period of time:

> *Inter*: Eva, what do you think about the girls in your class?
>
> *Mauritian girl*: It's good when I don't play they all – Holly and Kelly Ann came with me to ask me to play in the yard and I told them yes, and they let me play.
>
> *Local girl*: Like sometimes when Holly isn't here we – like I bring her to the place and we all get in a huddle and we decide what game we're playing.
>
> – P74/157, *Mauritian and local girls, Fourth class, School 6*

Two local children talking about reaching out to a newly arrived migrant girl reveal something of the politics that may arise in these situations. In this case, they show how they reached out in spite of (because of?) the fact that the child in question was being treated poorly by other local children:

> *Local girl 1*: I don't know, nobody does play with her out in the yard, me and Alison done it and play our games ...
>
> *Local girl 2*: So do I.
>
> *Local girl 1*: ... nobody plays with her.
>
> *Inter*: Yeah?

Local girl 2: I think it's quite mean.

Local girl 1: So do I, but me and Alison let her play a game.

Local girl 2: Some people say ...

Local girl 1: Yeah, some people say she copies your work and all but ...

Local girl 2: ... but I think they're only trying to get her into trouble.

Local girl 1: ... but once she copied me and again I said 'it's okay we'll leave it ...

Inter: Yeah.

Local girl 1: ... because you're only new like and you have to learn'.

– P239/318, *Two local girls, Fourth class, School 6*

In this extract, and in the one preceding it, the children use the phrase 'let her play' which is a revealing phrase. We might be tempted to take this as condescending and it may well be. However, to 'let someone play' is a common schoolyard term that reflects what happens when someone is admitted to an established (essentially conservative) peer group.

Willing to Get Along ... Positive but Qualified

In terms of the approach of local children towards new arrivals to their school, one clearly identifiable attitude is broadly positive, but one which is qualified in some way. One version of this view recognises difference positively or, at least, neutrally. Such differences seem to be recognised not on the basis of culture or nationality but on the basis of shared interests and temperament. Most commonly, this sees migrant children being regarded as 'quiet' or 'shy'. This can mean that at times they are evaluated quite positively.

Inter: Okay. And now there's lots of boys and girls in the school from different countries. What do you think about that?

Local girl 1: They're very kind they are ...

Local girl 2: Cos they're very like shy and all cos they came from different schools and all.

Local girl 1: Yeah and quiet.

Inter: Yeah? And have you got friends from different countries?

Local girl 1: Yea Alena, Tasha, Irina.

– P101/186, *Local girls, Fifth class, School 1*

Inter: Okay cool and what do you guys think that there's foreign kids, kids from all over the world in your school?

Local girl 1: They're alright, like they're some of them are nice, like most of them in the school, from like other countries are nice. Like I never heard them like being cheeky or anything, I think they're nice. Do you know the new girl that came here, she's in Sixth class, her name is, what's her name?

Inter: Danica?

Local girl 2: Yeah and like people when they join are very shy and then they just pop out of their shell, and like they're always very jolly and all, they're never let ...

Local girl 1: And like anytime you see Danica, when we're walking along in school, like she always says hiya and all, and she smiles at us and all, she's very nice. Because like when you get to know them they're very nice.

– P44/76, *Local girls, Fifth class, School 6*

These examples are both from girls. Boys express similar attitudes, but tend to use fewer words:

> *Inter*: Now, anyone new start in the class this year?
>
> *Local boy*: Yeah, Abdi. He's from Turkey. He's all right, like he's sound and all that.
>
> – P295, *Local boy, Sixth class, School 4*

Another version of a broadly open attitude which is qualified in some way is of the form 'it depends on how they behave'. Such views are more conditional than positive. They are, however, clearly distinguishable from the negative views we shall encounter later.

These very often seem to be based on some very specific negative experience (which has perhaps been over-generalised) and may be comparatively easy to work on in the sense of potential for reducing unsympathetic views.

> *Local girl 1*: Yeah, some of the kids we can cooperate, some of us can cooperate, some of them can't cooperate with us. So like say if you were from Nigeria, we wanted to play with you, we wanted to help you to find friends, you know if you were being bad to us, we're going to obviously be bad and we're not going to stand there and let you shout at us.
>
> *Local girl 2*: If she shouts at me I give cheek back because she has no business shouting at me, she doesn't know me.
>
> – P157/318, *Local girls, Fourth class, School 6*
>
> *Local girl 1*: No like, that's their choice, if they want to be bold they can be bold but we're only telling them not to get into trouble.
>
> *Inter*: And why – do you think that Etel [Hungarian girl] gets on well in your class?
>
> *Both*: Yeah, Etel's very good ...
>
> *Local girl 1*: ... she never gets into trouble.

Inter: Yeah and is she friends with everybody?

Both: Yeah.

Local girl 2: Like if she's – like if you say to her 'can I use your colours?', she'd say 'yeah any time' like you don't …

Local girl 1: You wouldn't get any of like 'oh no, there's too many people – oh no, I'm not letting anyone, oh no' like this and that.

Inter: Okay.

Local girl 2: … like making excuses like.

– P205/273, *Local girls, Fourth class, School 6*

The New Norm

There is evidence that the multi-cultural character of inner-city schools and neighbourhoods may be coming to be regarded by some teachers and pupils as normal. In the following extract, a teacher talks about her experience moving from a rural to an inner-city school:

Yeah, well, the interesting thing, I suppose is I've had senior classes in both schools but the children here, because it's an inner-city area, they'd be more used to having had children from other countries up along from First class or whatever when they started to come in. Whereas in the school I was in previously when I was in Fifth or Sixth class to get a child from abroad was a big deal, I mean not in a bad way, it's like a novelty, you know, whereas now it's just a given – oh where are you from? I don't think they really see difference, like, they know there's differences but they know they're different as well, it's not something that they see as a bad thing.

– *Teacher 3, Fourth class, School 3*

Of course, children will rarely talk about these issues in such a clear fashion, but a similar message often appears:

> ... all Romanian people live on my road.
>
> – P53, Local girl, Second class, School 5

> *Local boy*: It can be hard at the start because you don't know them but then when you get used to them and all then when they're in your class now then it can be pretty, it can be easy because you can talk to them all the time and like they're your friends.
>
> *Inter*: Do you ever forget that they're from different places?
>
> *Local boy*: Yeah. Because of the way they talk because the Dublin accents come out in them sometimes and you just think that they're Irish.
>
> – P223, Local boy, Sixth class, School 4

> *Local boy 1*: ... there's that guy from next door from Nigeria he's – Gabriel – we get along with him very well.
>
> *Local boy 2*: ... and Alexander and ...
>
> *Local boy 1*: ... and there's Alexander from Lithuania ...
>
> *Local boy 3*: ... yeah in our class.
>
> *Local boy 1*: ... and there is people from Poland that we know like. Some people from Poland only come over – there is a guy in Fifth class – he only come over and we got along with him straight away.
>
> – P98/169/175, Local boys, Sixth class, School 2

The following may sound like name-calling, but in the context of Dublin slang actually conveys a lot of warmth:

> ... the Latvo does mostly play chasing with us. She's kind of here all her life.
>
> – P309, Local girl, Fifth class, School 3

Opportunities at Yard Time

Yard time is the key period of unstructured and unsupervised play time in which migrant and local children are free to interact. As will be discussed later, a tendency towards separation is clearly marked, but on the other hand, cross-community peer groups also occur frequently. Although activities differ among girls and boys, some similar patterns emerge.

Children's accounts of who they play with at yard time, often given as a list of names (Owen, Carl, Ivan etc.), may reflect a bewildering diversity of nationalities. For confidentiality reasons, these are not reproduced here, but it worth pointing out that they are often corroborated by different children from the same play group when interviewed alone or in pairs. Such groups can also be observed in the school yard:

> The classes are not allowed to mix with each other and the children must play with their class or the other classes in their years. At a very broad level, it appears that the children mix quite well together with Irish children and international children involved in each football game.
>
> – Researcher field notes, Boys' school

Sport, especially football, plays an enormously important role in the social life of boys in school. There is always at least one game at yard time and football forms a constant topic of conversation in and out of the class. In one observation session in a boys' school, our field worker noted that when asked to produce pictures to illustrate concepts such as helpfulness, politeness, generosity and fun, most of the boys drew football and other sporting themes as demonstrations. Ideally, football can be an opportunity for intercultural interaction, as taking part in a game requires only basic language skills. In our observations, we noted many migrant children taking part in the lunchtime game. Here a Nigerian and local boy talk enthusiastically about the yard time game they have played in and won:

> *Local boy*: Cause one time when we were playing a team, they were winning us just by ...
>
> *Nigerian boy*: Two to three.
>
> *Local boy*: Two to three.
>
> *Nigerian boy*: And then we just won it. No it was actually two.
>
> *Local boy*: Not it was one all.
>
> *Nigerian boy*: Two.
>
> *Local boy*: It was one also, Harry got it was two to one to ...
>
> *Nigerian boy*: No Boyd, Boyd it's actually ...
>
> –P213/279, Local and Nigerian boys, Second class, School 4

For some migrant boys, football seems to offer an avenue of social inclusion and even prestige. The positive potential of sport is important, but it does seem to have limits in terms of whom and how it influences. Football is generally organised by the boys themselves and even when this is not so, it is often too rough and chaotic for many children regardless of ethnicity. Many children talked about how they dislike and avoid sports in the yard. Two second year boys explain a fairly extreme strategy they have adopted:

> *Local boy 1*: Some would play football.
>
> *Inter*: Okay.
>
> *Local boy 2*: And me and Ciaran would hide, wouldn't we?

Local boy 1: Oh yeah.

Local boy 2: Because we wouldn't want to get punched like.

Local boy 1: We'd be running like 'don't want to get punched' [*laughter*] or just duck.

Local boy 2: I'd say 'we're just going to the toilet' and never come out.

Inter: Never come out yeah?

Local boy 2: Yeah, until yard's over.

– P1/214, Local boys, Second class, School 4

As we noted in Chapter 4 many migrant children tend to be academically orientated and unused to the kinds of 'rough' neighbourhoods in which they find themselves living. Many find yard time sports rough, disorganised and aggressive:

Romanian boy: Well, I play with them, they play rough, like ...

Inter: Do they? What way do they play rough?

Romanian boy: They like, they get ye and if an accident, they hit ye with their legs.

– P136, Romanian boy, Second class, School 2

Of course, roughness is not the only reason that children do not engage in sport. As we discuss in the next chapter, opportunities for interaction are not always taken as some children find it quite difficult to become involved with the class and games in the yard:

Inter: And why would you like to play with the other boys?

Romanian boy: Like to play football, hide and seek, and other games.

Inter: And why can't you play football? [*Pause*] How do you get into a football match? Do you know? [*Pause*] Can you just go up to them? Or do they have to ask you?

Romanian boy: They don't call me to play with them.

– P138, Romanian boy, Fourth class, School 1

This uncertainty in how to become involved with a game was most prominent in schools where an adult did not supervise football games. In the absence of an adult gatekeeper, it was also more likely for some migrant boys to be actively excluded from games:

Inter: And what do you think of ... do you ever play football?

African boy: I don't really play.

Local boy: They don't let him play.

Inter: Why don't they let you play?

African boy: [*emotion in his voice*] I don't know.

Local boy: Because they say he's very annoying and all.

Inter: They say what?

Local boy: They say he's not playing, he wrecks your head and all.

Inter: Okay, and why do you think they say that?

African boy: I don't know.

Inter: And how does that make you feel, Badru?

African boy: Sad.

Inter: Yeah, and would you like to play football?

African boy: Yeah.

– P171, *African and local boys, Second class, School 1*

Social Interaction 1: Learning Together 101

The net effect of this seems to be three broad groupings during yard time: those who take part in the dominant lunchtime football match, those who do not get involved with sport and those who take part in alternative football games or other sports such as basketball. Research such as this is not designed to count exact numbers, but our impression would be that in proportion to the absolute numbers, migrants boy are less likely to be involved in the yard time football game as compared to local boys. One of the schools demonstrated this with particular clarity as the yard had two sections from which the boys could choose, the larger section where sports predominated and a smaller section with non-contact activities and basketball hoops. A teacher at the school explains:

> There are some kids who generally don't like to play football, it is not their thing to be running and chasing and playing football so you have to allow for them. The majority are out the front and that is by choice but if they want they can go to the back and there is somewhere safe and they can enjoy their break and not be hiding away somewhere away from everyone.... But it [the larger yard] is sectioned off, but each class had their own place to play in. Like Second class shouldn't be playing with Fourth class for safety and everything else. Well this is only in the front yard, in the back yard they can move around as much as they like. Because generally in front it is all football, we are better off having the smaller ones playing together and the bigger ones playing together, it just makes it fairer and safer. But that was the reason for that because out there is just so much football and there are a few boys who play chasing and things like that. And in the back yard it is just boys who prefer quieter things.
>
> – Teacher 2, Second class, School 2

A fieldworker studying the smaller yard noted that the majority of children in this yard were of migrant origin and local boys not known to 'cause trouble', boys with a reputation of being either studious and/or quiet. Relatively few instances of aggression were noted in this yard, even when basketball games were in play, and the boys were understood to play well together.

The larger yard in this school was similar to yards in other schools we visited. On first impression it appeared quite confused, but on closer inspection three main groupings could be discerned. The first was a large grouping, which engaged in football and was generally dominated by local boys but also included migrant boys. The second grouping consisted of small groups of boys, both migrant and local, who engaged in games such chasing and fantasy play. The third was a separate football game away from the main grouping which was dominated by migrant boys but also included local boys. This third group was not always present each day as it relied on the boys being provided with an extra ball to play with and free space in the yard. Thus, its existence relied on the discretion of the adult supervisors in the yard.

In all these groups, there were positive opportunities for interest-based relationships between children of different cultural backgrounds. While there may be some positive contact in yard time, given the little out of school contact reported to us, we may wonder whether such positive contact holds true beyond the yard life outside of school. Indeed, in many cases, interaction within sports and games also provided an opportunity for some dominant local boys to exclude others within the game, by not passing the ball to them, to insult them during 'pickies', or to stereotype some children as 'bad' players by ridiculing their football skills.

In the girls' schools, some similar patterns occur although the principal activities may vary. Once again, sport may be seen as too rough by some:

> *Filipino girl*: Yes you get sweaty and all. Do you know when they throw it and you have to catch it, if you catch it and just stand there they go all over.
>
> *Inter*: Okay, you were playing that game.

Filipino girl: Yes I played it before and I was running as fast as I could and I got sweaty and there was sweat all over me.

Inter: Do you think that the games are too ...

Nigerian girl: Harmful.

Inter: Is it that they are very strong and ...

Nigerian girl: Yes they are very strong.

– P26/05, *Filipino and Nigerian girls, Fourth class, School 3*

In the later years in these schools, team sport for girls in the yard is not as prominent, although many girls continue to play ball games such as basketball, dodge ball, throwing and passing games and other physical games such as skipping. The other main activity for girls in the senior years is talking in more or less established groups. Again, a similar pattern to the boys' yard can be observed with a minority of migrant children taking part in games and socialising with local children, but a majority staying in national or international groups. Here, two typical migrant girls discuss what they do during yard time:

Inter: What do you do then during the yard time?

Filipino girl: Talk.

Mauritian girl: We just talk.

Inter: Just talk and do you play your games, do you play games with the others or?

Mauritian girl: Yeah sometimes, but when they invite us to play.

Inter: Okay. So you said you talk about Mauritius, about your countries and where you come from, okay.

Mauritian girl: And we also play ask me what? I ask some question and ...

Filipino girl: I answer.

Inter: What kind of question like?

Mauritian girl: Like Geography question.

– *P112/87, Filipino and Mauritian girls, Fourth class, School 3*

As with football, the group activities that girls engage in (such as skipping and basketball) are crucial opportunities for intercultural interaction However, the quote above clearly highlights mechanisms of inclusion and exclusion in operation in the school yard, as the two girls wait to be invited to participate in yard time games.

Friendships

In some cases, play groupings at yard time can be fluid and transient. For example, they may form opportunistically on the spot for the sake of a game. More often, there will be more enduring connections among children who form close friendships, including, occasionally, the strongest of all bonds between peers, a best friendship.

The following few extracts are from cases in which warmer friendships have developed between migrant and local children:

I get on really well with Victoria [Romanian girl].

– *P315, Local girl, Fourth class, School 3*

I get along with Abdi [Turkish Boy] sometimes Abdi he's my best friend.

– *P28, Local boy, Sixth class, School 4*

Inter: Do you have any friends who are from different countries?

Local girl: Friends from different countries. Well I have Aluna [Kenyan girl] in there.

Inter: Yeah?

Local girl: Yeah. She's a really good friend though.

– P177, Local girl, Fourth class, School 7

It is also possible to detect genuine warmth and friendship in the sadness which some children express over the breaking of relationships with changes in school.

Local girl: And I'll miss her when we go to secondary.

Inter: Yeah, you're going to different secondary schools, are you?

Polish girl: Yeah she's going to Westin and I might go to James' or the Temple.

– P243/243, Local and Polish girls, Sixth class, School 6

Inter: Where is Alexandra from?

Local girl: She's from Romania and she was the most nicest person ever. When she went off it was horrible.

– P70, Local girl, Fourth class, School 3

Almost in passing, children will mention minor details from their lives which reveal quite close bonds between them. In the following extract, a local child talks about walking home from school with her Romanian friend:

> I walk her home and take her right up to her door and make sure she gets in okay, and then I run back, me sister waits for me at the corner and I run back to her.
>
> – P291, Local girl, Fourth class, School 1

In the following extract, an Irish child talks about a similar arrangement between two local children and a Hungarian girl in her class:

> I think everyday Kelly and Hannah used to knock for her at about eight o'clock in the morning and then they used

to go to school. When they'd come home from school they'd fight and then you'd say ah I'm not knocking for you in the morning and they'd end up knocking for each other. But Kelly and Hannah always have to knock for Yllona in the mornings. Because they get up earlier and Yllona watches telly if nobody knocks for her.

– P53, Local girl, Sixth class, School 5

A few children from different cultural backgrounds talk about visiting each other at home. Mostly this involves those who live close to one another and have known each other since the very beginning of schooling. Sometimes, out of school contact can also be based on a coincidence, as in this example:

Inter: So who are some of your friends that you play with after school?

Local girl: Erika and Zee, and Katie and Erika's friend.

Inter: And does Zee [Romanian] live near you? Do you guys live near each other?

Local girl: No, but my Godmother has this daughter and she lives beside Esther, and I just come over.

Inter: Oh, so you guys get to play after school sometimes? And do you know her friends for her neighbourhood? And does she know your friends?

Local girl: I know her friends but she doesn't know my friends.

– P270, Local girl, First class, School 5

Discussion

We encountered a range of attitudes among local children towards their migrant peers. Among these, we detected a definite positive strain. We suspect that, in many instances, these attitudes were held at the instigation of adults, but nonetheless they appear to be genuine and can usually be distinguished from weaker forms of 'politically correct' responding. In the qualitative element of *Adapting to Diversity* (Smith, Darmody, McGinnity and Byrne, 2009), the majority of Irish students were found to express similarly positive views about migrants to Ireland.

Sympathy for isolated migrant peers can lead to local children reaching out to, or attempting to involve, the individuals concerned. Although these endeavours may be short-lived and produce little by way of long-term friendship, they can be valuable for the individuals involved. Where more long-term friendships do not develop, this often appears to be the result of underlying differences in interest and temperament, rather than superficiality or ill will. The importance of shared interests is also underlined by the way in which local children qualify their positive attitudes by awareness of these differences. Children who are positively disposed towards newcomers to the school also show an awareness that getting along is a two-way street. The lessons would appear to be that children will be more likely to get along if they can find shared interests, and that responsibility for the development and maintenance of relationships cannot all come from one side.

The unstructured play of yard time reveals much about the nature of social interaction in multi-cultural schools. On the one hand, many genuine opportunities are open to newcomer students to make friends and to gain status through sport and yard time play. On the other hand, those opportunities are limited to a minority of children and may not easily transfer beyond the school yard. This is not a criticism or even a limitation, but something we have to bear in mind when assessing the genuinely positive value that sport and games can have in promoting positive inter-cultural relations.

Finally, we can note that in spite of a prevalent sense of distance and the occurrence of quite intense hostility which will be explored in the following chapters, close and warm friendships between migrant and local children can develop of their own accord in a small number of cases.

Chapter 6

Social Interaction 2: Distance and Separateness

> *Indifference to children from other cultures is generally marked by separateness, a tendency to stay with what is familiar, for children to simply pass one another by. We believe that this kind of indifference has a dynamic and energy of its own. It is not simply a neutral point between positive and negative. We also believe that this phenomenon is the key characteristic of inter-cultural relations in the primary schools we visited and is crucial for understanding the future of inter-cultural relations in these schools and the communities they serve. We predict that if these children carry their experiences into adulthood then we will have 'parallel' rather than integrated communities.*

This chapter is divided into a description of 'separateness' and its characteristics, a discussion of some contributing factors and a brief consideration of some of the more obvious immediate consequences in the classroom.

Keeping Separate

When children are able to mix freely, there is a marked tendency for local children to play among themselves and for migrant children to interact with children from their own ethnic background or with other migrants. Local children talk about this in a number of ways. Most common is the view that migrant children are nice and cause little trouble. With this, there is a fairly bare assertion that they simply do not play with them:

Inter: And so what do you think about like the foreign kids coming into the school like, is it kind of a good thing or a bad thing kind of?

Local girl 1: It's a good thing like because they have to come over and learn like.

Inter: Yeah.

Local girl 1: To learn.

Inter: So you think they'd come and they'd learn like, yeah? But like would you play with them ...

Local girl 1: Yeah.

Local girl 2: No.

Inter: ... or would you just play with your own friends?

Local girl 2: Play with me own friends but like if they were really, really, really nice like I might do.

– P78/274, Local girls, Fifth class, School 7

No I'm not saying they don't fit in like. I play with them no problem. But they just play with other people from their own country and things.

– P181, Local girl, Fifth class, School 3

Local girl: Some of them [children from different countries] are nice.

Inter: Yeah?

Local girl: But I never played with any of them.

Inter: How come?

Local girl: Because I just play with all me friends, you know, me friends.

– P323, Local girl, Fourth class, School 6

In a similar vein are statements that migrant children just fit in, are rarely seen or heard, are almost invisible:

> They're sound, they don't make trouble they don't stand out, like they're grand
>
> – P190, Local boy, Sixth class, School 1

> *Local boy 1*: Fine they're fine in the yard but you wouldn't really notice them.
>
> *Local boy 2*: They're there alright but they're real quiet.
>
> *Local Boy 1*: They don't really stand out.
>
> –P113/190, *Local boys, Sixth class, School 1*

In all of these statements, there is a sense of normality about the keeping apart, a neutral acceptance that it is just the way things are. As a further example, in the following extract a local girl explains why she thinks migrant children do not attend a children's disco organised locally:

> *Local girl*: They wouldn't really mix with anybody because they don't like, if they went to the disco people would be just staring at them saying who are they and stuff like that.
>
> *Inter*: How come?
>
> *Local girl*: Because they don't really like hang around with people that go to the disco like. They wouldn't hang around with Ava or anything like that. They would probably [*inaudible*] and Katie and they'd just go into a corner and they'd stay there because they just don't hang around with any of us. It's not that we don't want to, it's just they don't fit in like.
>
> – P181, *Local girl, Fifth class, School 3*

Social Interaction 2: Distance and Separateness   111

On occasion, slightly more annoyance is evident, especially a sense that inter-cultural communication is awkward or embarrassing.

> *Inter*: Is it easy or hard …
>
> *Local boy 1*: Easy.
>
> *Inter*: … to be friend with people from other countries?
>
> *Local boy 1*: Hard.
>
> *Local boy 2*: Hard.
>
> *Inter*: Hard. Okay, we'll let Bernard go on that one there for a minute. Why do you think it's hard?
>
> *Local boy 2*: Because they kind of just walk away and all when you ask them.
>
> *Inter*: They walk away?
>
> *Local boy 2*: Yeah, when it's kind of just like awkward.
>
> – P37/82, *Local boys, Senior Infants class, School 7*

More direct irritation can also be detected at times:

> *Local girl*: Why would they like know you well if they won't go apart from each other?
>
> *Inter*: Okay.
>
> *Local girl*: … they're like glue people.
>
> *Inter*: So there in a small group by themselves like?
>
> *Local girl*: Glue people.
>
> –P277, *Local girl, Fifth class, School 7*

Teachers offer a slightly different perspective on the same phenomenon, but again they often seem to regard this separateness as the natural state of affairs:

> ... that is kind of universal in most schools, foreign nationals hang out together whether they are Polish, Romanian, Hungarian, I just don't know how that can be changed, you know, what can we do as teachers to try and change that. Or if there is any point in even trying, it is human nature, I don't know ... Just go with what feels comfortable.
>
> – *Teacher 5, Sixth class, School 6*

There is also evidence that pressure to stay apart can come from the migrant side as well. In the following example, a teacher talks about the way in which migrant children will seek to be on the same teams during PE:

> ... that they don't have a problem working with other children, that they are actually quite popular in the class. But I do notice that there is a tendency that they all stick together, especially during PE, they rearrange themselves to be able to get into their team and are counting to see how I was splitting them and then they rearrange, so it is very clever.
>
> – *Teacher 4, Fifth class, School 6*

In the following extract, a migrant pupil gives an interesting insight into how the mechanics of separateness work. She describes how the local children, when they feel like it, will talk in such a way as to exclude migrant children:

> *Mauritian girl*: ... sometimes the other girls, the Irish girls, because we're from here, they just talk to us now the way, sometimes that when they don't want us to be there on their table and everything. That's alright sometimes they like me, sometimes their mood are not right, but that's ok.
>
> [Other topic]

Inter: What did you say, sometimes they talk ... is it they talk about you or ... I didn't hear what you said properly?

Mauritian girl: No, you know the way that you talk to me in this way and you talk to her another way, like louder and ...

Inter: Ok so they talk to you in a different way, and is it in a nice way or ...

Mauritian girl: Sometimes in a nice way but when their mood is not right, something happened maybe at home or they got in trouble with teacher, then they don't talk to anyone.

– P112, Mauritian girl, Fourth class, School 3

The separateness between local and migrant children is also reflected in the fact that they see very little of each other outside of school, even in cases where mixed play groups exist.

Local girl: There are lots of different nationalities in my class and then there is Wei from China who is not in school anymore but there is still a Chinese girl in the class though.

Inter: Do you ever hang out with them outside of school too?

Local girl: No not that much, only Wei, but I haven't been in her house in a while, because I don't really see her that much anymore.

– P293, Local girl, Fifth class, School 7

Of course, it is not necessarily unusual for children who play together in school not to meet too often outside of school. However, such contact outside of school is an important part of the picture as we try to understand social interaction in the classroom between children from different cultural backgrounds.

Finally, a sense of the separateness is implied in a phenomenon which we can call 'model friendships' which occurs when a best friendship between a local and a migrant child is referred to frequently, or in detail, by other people in the school. It is basically a 'celebrity friendship', the novelty of which draws attention to its relatively rarity. Here, for example, two local girls talk about the friendship that exists between another local girl and a Polish girl in their class:

> *Local girl 1*: She was real kind and everyone was saying hello and Carla was ...
>
> *Local girl 2*: Her best friend – she has a picture of Carla in her pencil case, Anka.
>
> *Inter*: Oh yeah?
>
> *Local girl 1*: Yeah. I don't even know her real name.
>
> *Local girl 2*: Yeah but we're getting to know her, we're all getting to know her.
>
> *Local girl 1*: Yeah we're all getting to know her.
>
> *Inter*: Okay.
>
> *Local girl 2*: She's nice to talk to.
>
> *Local girl 1*: Carla knows her because before she started, she started talking to her in town for some reason.
>
> *Inter*: Yeah.
>
> *Local girl 1*: They are best friends in school.
>
> – *P164/254, Local girls, Sixth class, School 6*

Factors Contributing to Separateness

There are many forces at work keeping migrant and local children apart. Some of these relate to differences in background, home life and language ability. Some relate to features of the organisation of school and community life and to the kinds of assumptions that are brought to the interaction. Children may be only dimly aware

Social Interaction 2: Distance and Separateness

of some of these issues, if at all. In this section, we look at evidence of factors keeping children separate that emerged in our research, all the time bearing in mind that all actors in the situation will have limited awareness of the full range and extent of influences at work.

Cultural and language differences are of enormous importance. Aside from these, many other forces are at work. One of the first barriers that we have touched on already is the fact that these children are quite different from one another in many respects, both in attitude and in general outlook. As one teacher explains:

> Yes I suppose you make your friends for whatever reason, you have got things in common or you have the same personality or you like the same things, you are both good at dancing, you know, their mams are friends and you play outside the school, that is what makes it I think. They will tolerate each other and be nice to each other but I don't think you can forge friendships where you have to sit beside somebody.
>
> – *Teacher 5, Sixth class, School 6*

The following incident is revealing in that it shows clearly the effect of having different interests alongside inter-cultural differences. In this case, a local girl talks about how she was friends with a girl from Mauritius but is no longer so due to the fact that the girl now plays with more academic friends:

Local girl 1: Yeah, but like she's not really my friend.

Local girl 2: No.

Inter: Is she not, how come?

Local girl 1: I don't know.

Local girl 2: The first day she joined she was. She was scarlet.

Inter: Yeah.

Local girl 2: So we all helped her.

Inter: That's nice.

Local girl 1: Like she likes to play with brainy people ...

Local girl 2: And we're not brainy.

Local girl 1: We're not brainy at all.

Inter: That's not true.

Local girl 1: It is, ask me a sum.

– P144/297, Local girls, Fourth class, School 6

The issue of academic ethos comes up again and again:

Local boy 1: Mainly all of them are a bit different. Like cause that – like Bur and Michael are a bit different as well.

Local boy 2: What you'd call nerds. You make it easy,

Local boy 1: A bit like that,

Inter: Yeah?

Local boy 1: Michael – Bur is but Michael is a bit – he's a bit weird as well.

– P98/175, Local boys, Sixth class, School 6

As well as exhibiting less interest in academic matters, local children tend to enjoy a lot more freedom during out of school hours, as well as having a more confrontational attitude towards authority. The way in which common interests and attitudes can unite or separate children is revealed with particular clarity in the following extract in which an Irish girl who moved to Dublin is being interviewed with her Russian friend:

Local girl: I don't know, see when I first came to school all my best friends they all moved ...

Inter: Okay.

Local girl: ... they were all from – like my first best friend was from a different country ...

Inter: Okay.

Local girl: ... so I don't know it's just ...

Inter: Do you think they're more like you then?

Local girl: ... yeah, I don't know, it's just that my best friends are other people who come to Ireland ...

Inter: Yeah.

Local girl: ... because a lot of people from here are real Dubliners and I'm not a real Dubliner so ...

Inter: Okay yeah.

Local girl: ... that's why I probably fit in better like.

Inter: Is it hard to get on with like real Dubliners, that kind of idea?

Local girl: Yeah.

Inter: Yeah, because what would they be like?

Local girl: It's like getting on their case or something 'cause ...

Inter: Okay.

Russian girl: They are kind of more powerful or something.

Local girl: ... yeah ...

Inter: More powerful?

Local girl: ... like they're right or something.

Inter: Okay, yeah. So do you think like do they have like more attitude or something?

Local girl: Yeah.

> *Russian girl*: Probably yeah because they're used to here but like some people aren't.
>
> *Local girl*: They could maybe talk back to a teacher and get in trouble ...
>
> *Inter*: Okay.
>
> *Local girl*: ... like I would faint if I talked back [*laughter*].
>
> *Russian girl*: Me too.
>
> – P14/322, *Local and Russian girls, Fifth class, School 7*

Another major factor keeping children apart is the conservative nature of peer groups. Groups tend to form early on and can be difficult both to join and to break out of. The formation of such groups may or may not have anything to do with ethnicity – groups with mixed ethnic composition seem to follow exactly the same rules. However given that groups will tend to form early on, building on shared interests and pre-existing friendships, the very nature of play groups is a force which will tend to keep local and migrant children apart.

> There is a few who, if they got the chance, they'd go together because they have been in other classes together, you know junior infants and senior infants before so they naturally know those kids so they would go to them quicker I suppose.
>
> – *Teacher1, Second class, School 2*

Membership of playgroups is often 'policed' such that children ensure that all members of the group join in and monitor who the others play with.

> *Romanian girl*: I play with Gordana [Kosovar girl] too.
>
> *Inter*: You play with Gordana too. And what's the best thing to play?

Indian girl: And she playing all days with Pearl and Katie and Ava [three Irish girls].

Inter: Okay.

Indian girl: But we don't let her.

Inter: You don't let her. Why don't you let her?

Indian girl: Because we don't like Pearl and Katie and Ava.

Inter: Okay and why don't you like them?

Romanian girl: I like them …

Indian girl: Because Kiki [Egyptian girl] won't let us.

– P172/265, *Romanian and Indian girls, Senior Infants class, School 7*

This kind of in-group monitoring is rarely discussed so directly. Very often it emerges in off-hand comments, such as in the following extract in which two girls explain why a girl in their class does not play with them:

We do always ask her but she doesn't like … she plays with her friend, because she doesn't want to get into trouble.

– P4/137/320, *Local girls, Fourth class, School 6*

The conservative power of existing friendships networks is also revealed in teachers' accounts of the difficulty in intervening to create friendships for new arrivals:

Inter: And do you think moving desks and things like that have influenced friendships in any way? Like if Vanessa is at a table do you think she would be better friends with people at the table?

Teacher: Not really at this stage, they know who they are friendly with and they tolerate her but they have friends, they are in little cliques.

– Teacher 5, Sixth class, School 6

Finally, one other contributing factor worth mentioning is that outside of school the children often live in different areas. This is obviously particularly important in accounting for the infrequent out-of-school contact. Bearing in mind that comparatively short distances can seem quite large to children, the fact that children who go to school together will also sometimes live in different parts of their community is an issue that can also separate them:

… and they're in rented accommodation … Just physically they're not together, so they're not playing together and not mixing …

– Teacher 8, Senior Infants class, School 7

… say for example the Dublin children, by and large, most of them would come from the flats across the road, they live next door, they're out playing together in the evenings. That is their little group of friends; they still get on with the other children.

– Teacher 3, Fourth class, School 3

Consequences in the Classroom

The fact that migrant and local children in the same class are generally keeping apart from one another and moving along separate 'lines' can create the potential for misunderstanding and lack of communication.

One phenomenon which occurs is that of suspected hostility, a perception that behind apparently neutral actions lie hostile intentions. It is hard to show conclusively that this is related directly to separateness, but it does appear to create the conditions in which this can easily happen. The following is a typical example of suspected hostility:

Nigerian boy: When I wanted to play with his stuff he wouldn't let me.

Inter: He wouldn't let you? Why not?

Nigerian boy: Because I think he was jealous I was new or something.

– P271, Nigerian boy, Second class, School 5

On the other side of the coin are positive feelings of sympathy and compassion which remain latent, apparently because of the awkwardness of expressing them:

Local girl: See they don't know what we're kind of like.

Inter: Yeah?

Local girl: Even though they've been here for ages, they don't know what we can do and all but we wouldn't hop on them like, we just stick up for them …

– P308, Local girl, Fifth class, School 7

Discussion

Though not as striking or dramatic as some of the very positive or negative incidents we relate in other parts of this book, we think that the experience of separateness is more representative and characteristic of intercultural relations in these classrooms and resonates with other Irish evidence. A tendency for newcomers to socialize among themselves was also noted by both teachers and students in the focus group element of *Adapting to Diversity* (Smith, Darmody, McGinnity and Byrne, 2009). Molcho, Kelly, Gavin and Nic Gabhainn (2008) also noted that non-UK immigrant students tend to have narrower circles of friends. From the present study, we get a strong sense that separateness is not random, but is motivated by the personal preferences of individual actors in the classroom and school setting. There is a will to stay with what is comfortable and familiar. There is a sense that, for many, this is considered normal, the way things are: 'It's just they don't fit in'. 'It is human nature'. The implications of these observations may be far-reaching and may do much to set the tone for the future of inter-cultural relations in Ireland, as one of adjacency rather than integration. Indifference is also a very important part of the background for understanding prejudice in the classroom. While in some sense, inert, it may contribute to an environment of negative inter-ethnic relations by creating an atmosphere in which prejudice can be allowed to happen. There is also a sense in which we can think of the lack of intercultural dialogue among children as being a valuable opportunity missed for all parties. We will argue in the final chapter that separateness is one of the main issues that policy interventions need to target.

Having said that, even the most cursory consideration of possible contributing factors contained in this chapter will give us cause for reflection. Differences in social values, lack of shared interests and the conservative nature of peer groups are all powerful forces helping to keep children apart. Promoting positive integration, rather than mere tolerance, is a profound challenge which should be understood as related to, but separate from, attempts to address the more outright negative social phenomena which we will consider in the next chapter.

Chapter 7

Social Interaction 3: Prejudice, Bullying and Their Consequences

Negative ethnic relationships between children of different cultural groups are marked by feelings of self-importance, ignorance, jealousy, aggression, and insulting and derisory behaviour. In this chapter, we look initially at children's general ethnocentrism and prejudice towards migrants and then move on to look at more specific racial name-calling and bullying that is directed towards classmates. Finally, we document some of the serious consequences of racial bullying.

As discussed in Chapter 2, the relevant literature suggests that awareness of ethnicity and racial prejudice can emerge much earlier in childhood than most adults realise. In our research, we found that these issues had arisen in one form or another in all schools we visited, and even among the youngest children taking part. The picture is complex but we can outline the main features as follows:

- Ethnocentric beliefs expressing, either stated or implied, superiority of the native national group and the inadequacy of various out-groups were very common. This should not surprise us as such beliefs are commonplace among adults from all walks of life. Such beliefs form an important background for approaching children's understanding of migration.
- Some children have quite well-developed negative stereotypes of adult migrants to Ireland. Not all children expressed a view

on this, and many do not seem to even show an interest. However, in one of the seven schools that we visited, such negative stereotypes were particularly frequent and aggressive.

- Several migrant children in all schools had experienced name-calling and bullying in some form. Some of this may be part of the everyday roughness of schools and inner-city schools in particular. It can sometimes be difficult to differentiate, but alongside this there was also a definite strand of racial bullying evident.

- Reactions to racial bullying varied, but in some cases there was clear evidence of psychological harm.

Ethnocentrism

Ethnocentrism refers to a widespread tendency to see one's own group as superior while belittling or showing contempt for other groups. Within the Irish context, there are common stereotypes that present Ireland as a land of wealth and opportunity on the one hand, and typify the non-western world as consistently poverty-stricken, famished, war-torn, depressed and undeveloped on the other. People who have ethnocentric outlooks on the world are rarely emotional about them – at least until seriously challenged. Ethnocentrism tends to reveal itself by the kinds of assumptions people make when talking about the world around them – for example, that we might reasonably expect someone from Africa to be in awe of an indoor toilet or a mobile phone. Such views are easily fed by media portrayals of humanitarian disasters.

As a brief aside, it is worth mentioning that in our work with older children (Gilligan et al., 2010), migrant teenagers in Ireland often express annoyance with views of the world that they encounter here. We refer to this study here because teenagers will perceive those views with greater clarity and express their feelings about them with greater force than younger children:

> For instance, like there was a religion class, and they were discussing the Darfur problem and people started

coming out with some stupid ideas and really big images and all that. And there's a genocide and all that – well I think that's a whole lot of rubbish because the whole idea is just the same as the troubles between Northern Ireland and the Republic of Ireland and there's an extreme group in the region like that IRA and they are just going doing all that kind of nonsense. And there's people they're making a big image and you know a bad image of the whole thing and this and they comes up with some things they hear in the media which can be like 90 per cent of it is wrong ...

– *Sudanese youth, male, 16-years-old*

... they think everyone who is in Africa has HIV. Some people don't even want to touch you, like if they found out you're from Africa, stupid things like that.

– *Mozambican youth, female, 17-years-old*

In the present work, we found that such views were already well developed among many primary school children. Although Ireland has experienced migration from a breathtaking diversity of countries in a relatively short period of time, the stereotypical picture is that all migrants are from Africa (Nigeria) which is poor, famished and war-torn, or from former-Soviet republics (Romania) which are grim, cold, depressing and in a permanent economic slump. Stereotypes about Asians (Chinese) are less developed and more confused, but often relate to Chinese take-aways which have been a long-standing feature of fast food outlets in the inner-city.

When asked their opinions about different countries, children will often focus on physical characteristics ('their skin is black', 'their faces are pale') or on the weather. However, the ethnocentric strain is clearly present:

There's always like fighting over there [China].

– *P52, Local girl, Fifth class, School 6*

No we're much richer, they're like very, very poor.

– *P111, Local girl, Sixth class, School 6*

Africa is poor but they can move to Dublin.

– *P72, Local boy, Second class, School 4*

[Africans] ... just haven't got houses.

– *P127, Local girl, Sixth class, School 3*

Romania always has wars and all.

– *P216, Local boy, Second class, School 2*

Local girl 1: And they're [Africans] poor, and I'm not poor. And they have no shoes, and I have shoes. And like ...

Local girl 2: We have to waste our money on them.

– *P30/62, Local girls, Fifth class, School 6*

... like at the end of the day they [migrants] have come over 'cause some of them there's wars and all going on in their country and there's no jobs or food and all.

– *P234, Local girl, Fifth class, School 7*

Because they have to walk miles to get food. The shop is only around the corner from us. But like they don't have money or anything but they get a job over here and work.

– *P76, Local girl, Fifth class, School 6*

... like you'd get, at least like some people in Africa like don't get presents even though it's their birthday because they have no money to buy anyone presents so like ...

– *P273, Local girl, Fourth class, School 6*

Social Interaction 3: Prejudice, Bullying and Their Consequences

These kinds of representations of the world are easily fed by images of war and famine that charities use to raise money in schools.

> *Local girl 1*: ... poor over there, like do you ever see the ads for Trócaire? We give money to them in the Trócaire boxes we do.
>
> *Inter*: Yeah?
>
> *Local girl 2*: Yeah, and like sometimes we give them – we always give them clothes.
>
> – P78/274, Local girls, Fourth class, School 7
>
> *Inter*: What about people who live in Nigeria? Here's Nigeria, in Africa.
>
> *Local girl 1*: They could be very different to us because they've no food ...
>
> *Local girl 2*: Yeah.
>
> *Inter*: What do you mean they've no food?
>
> *Local girl 1*: ... like they're poor and then like you know like the way we get the Trócaire boxes and we bring money over to them, you put it into the Trócaire box and like there's an ad on the telly and I can't watch it, it's too sad, because like they're all – they have little kids and all and there's all flies flying around them and eating their food ...
>
> – P205/273, Local girls, Fourth class, School 6

Such stereotypes of the developing world are almost universal and can be found among quite well-educated adults. In primary school, they are also not confined to local children:

> *Inter*: OK, so do you think you are the same or different from people from India?

Nigerian boy: Different.

Inter: In what way are you different?

Nigerian boy: Because in India they use coconuts as cups to drink.

– P339, *Nigerian boy, Second class, School 2*

Negative Attitudes and Beliefs about Adult Migrants

As we said in the opening chapter, migration has been a trigger for major demographic change, affecting areas such as Dublin's north inner-city profoundly. In our interviews, local children naturally tend to focus on their school life and the migrant children that they have known. However, on some occasions they talked about the broader social context and related stories about migrant adults and the wider community. These stories arose in some school contexts more than others, and often reflect very salient or stereotypical aspects of the changes which migration is perceived to have brought. One school in particular, School 6, an all girls' school, seemed to be particularly rife with negative stories about migrants. Although negative stereotypical images of adult migrants occurred across the range of years and schools that we visited, children in Fourth, Fifth and Sixth classes of School 6 produced them more frequently and in a more extreme degree than children in other schools that participated. We will return to the thorny question of why such views should be in particular evidence at School 6 at the end of this section. Many, though not all examples, in this section are taken from School 6.

Negative stereotypical images of adult migrants held by children are often closely associated with beliefs held by sections of the adult population of Ireland since the increase of migration into Ireland. In analysis of Irish adult survey data on attitudes to 'minorities' ('in particular those groups of people whose arrival in Ireland especially since the mid-1990s altered the perceived homogeneity of the population'), O'Connell and Winston (2006) noted that between 1997 and 2002 the percentage of people who

Social Interaction 3: Prejudice, Bullying and Their Consequences

thought that there were 'Too many' minorities more than doubled from just under 10 per cent to just over 20 per cent. In the same study, they note that the most common negative beliefs held about 'minorities' were that they abuse social welfare and increase unemployment. Among the children in our study we observed two common beliefs related to these adult outlooks. One concerned the idea of Ireland being taken over by migrants, and the other of jobs going to migrants which should go to Irish people:

> There's no room for Irish people.
>
> – P312, Local girl, Fourth class, School 6

> ... Dublin's going to be taken over by them.
>
> – P62, Local girl, Fifth class, School 6

> I don't mind an' all but ... people I know aren't getting' their jobs, like an' people from other countries get them.
>
> – P103, Local boy, Sixth class, School 2

> They are taking over our jobs.
>
> – P137, Local girl, Fourth class, School 6

A belief which we encountered frequently was the idea that migrants, particularly migrant beggars, often fraudulently seek charity or assistance:

> But some people like, like do you know all them Romanian people and all they just do go around in all different clothes and they do like to sit on the street and begging for money and all. And once I saw them around, I think it was Busáras [central bus station] and they were like sitting down begging for money with a blanket over the baby and the Garda saw them so the Garda took the money and they said, here don't be begging on the street so they went. And sometimes they can get very greedy with their money, because they do

be on the streets, and I ... like I saw them doing this they empty their cup out when it's full, they put them, they hide them in their pockets and they say please I have no money, and they ask for more, and they just keep getting it, and then they do have more money than us and we do be giving them it.

– *P76, Local girl, Fifth class, School 6*

Sometimes there's a girl lives down the road from me and like me Ma left the clothes down one day and you know like because you put a sticker on it so they can collect it in the morning, and once my Ma saw the girl, like it wasn't from our house, it was from a different house, taking the clothes. And like it wasn't for her, it was for the children and people, and she took them. And you know it was for them to send away to the other people that have no clothes.

– *P44, Local girl, Fifth class, School 6*

Some people come over here and they have like way better stuff, like from Nigeria and they come over and there's like loads of stuff like, they can get money quicker and all, food quicker.

– *P44, Local girl, Fifth class, School 6*

And I'm not saying, but do you ever see them over here, they're loaded like. And do you ever see the people that beg, there does be loads of them.

– *P30, Local girl, Fifth class, School 6*

Local girl 1: There's these Paki people [*laughter*] like not next door like about two doors down and my Ma like – they got very like, like ...

Local girl 2: Like bold.

Local girl 1: ... because when my Ma left her hoover outside me door because it wasn't working and she left it outside for the bin men to take it and they took it into their house.

Inter: Okay.

Local girl 1: And one time me Ma threw out old bedding and they took that into their houses and it was left lying outside the street and then they brought it in. And like one time my Ma was walking down the road from work and she was at her house, she could see it and all like me Ma's house, and then the Romanians – do you know them recycling bags, the green ones? – they were in me Ma's letterbox to use and the girl must have had none, the Romanian, and she took them out of me Ma's letterbox and brought them into her house and me Ma saw them so me Ma put the latch on the door and knocked in and said – and they go – and they said 'we don't speak no English', you know, messing.

Local girl 2: Yeah.

Local girl 1: And my Ma banged down the door and they came out and she goes 'where's the girl that came in a minute ago with the green bags? They were my bags.' and she was able to understand her like that then and then she went in and gave them to her and me Ma said 'if you take anything like that again ...'.

– P205/273, *Local girls, Fourth class, School 6*

Representations also emerged which associate migrants with trouble and criminal danger:

And we were in the house and the baby was playing on the floor and we brought her into bed and she fell asleep straight away and we came out and we were watching a film and we lowered the film down because we heard banging and the lights on me Ma's friend's ceiling nearly came off because the man up top was killing her and he was a foreigner and the fella that owns them came up and he was afraid to hit him. And if it happened with any of us they'd throw us out.

– P4, Local girl, Fourth class, School 6

I don't like them because it's mad dangerous when they're with you. Because you know when you're Mas and all were smaller it wasn't dangerous 'cause none of them were over, but now it's much more dangerous, everyone is getting shot and all, since they all moved over, and it's all of them. And everyone's getting kidnapped and it's all like the Romanians and the blacks.

– P62, Local girl, Fifth class, School 6

And some people like foreigners and that, there's loads of foreigners and they do start loads of trouble, and 'cause like you do hear them in the night and you do hear them fighting and roaring and shouting, just say like two o'clock in the morning, people does be trying to sleep.

– P76, Local girl, Fifth class, School 6

Local girl 1: Because like you know like foreigners, see how they pick pockets.

Inter: They do what …?

Local girl 1: All foreigners pick pockets.

Local girl 2: She means like they rob shops. Like I know the way them girls with the thing on their head and they wrap this yoke around their head. They bring a huge bag with them because they rob out of shops. That is what the tinkers does.

– P55/305, Local girls, Fourth class, School 6

Local girl 1: Like 'cause I'm always saying like it's disgraceful, every morning you wake up there's a murder, there's like after been a crash, a stabbing, a shooting, it's disgraceful it is.

Inter: Yeah.

Local girl 1: Like someone dies every morning and every night.

Inter: Okay. So you said you don't really like the foreign people coming over?

Local girl 2: No.

Local girl 1: No, but I'm not saying like that it's all ...

Inter: Yeah?

Local girl 1: ... it's the foreign people, I'm just saying that every morning you wake up ...

Inter: Yeah.

Local girl 1: ... and like you're after hearing about murders.

Local girl 2: It's all the foreign people that's killing us like, do you know, in the murders.

Inter: Okay yeah, yeah so you think things are a little more dangerous, do you?

Local girl 1: Like I don't know where they got that idea 'oh yeah, we're going to go over to Ireland' ...

Inter: Yeah.

Local girl 2: And take their land or something.

– P78/274, Local girls, Fifth class, School 7

Local girl 1: And they carry knifes and all in their socks don't they? The coloured fellas. And they do be all down the [district name], and don't they carry knives in their stockings? The area [district name], but none of us like, it's all like coloured people.

Local girl 2: You see them walking through and you can see, you know the way they wear their stockings tucked in, and you can't really see the knife, it's skinny, you can see the knife.

– P30/62, *Local girls, Fifth class, School 6*

The last two extracts reveal another aspect of children's negative beliefs about migrants and crime, namely, that such beliefs can sometimes have an exaggerated, almost 'folklorish' dimension. Again, such beliefs were most frequent and most dramatic in School 6. Accusations of kidnapping were common:

I think I don't like them because there are too many of them and since there are too many there is loads of kids getting kidnapped and all that.

– P137, *Local girl, Fourth class, School 6*

And they kidnap us and that's not fair and they're bold. They're mean and all like.

– P312, *Local girl, Fourth class, School 6*

Local girl: … some of them are kidnappers.

Inter: Okay, what do you mean by that?

Local girl: Like some of them, like get children and they throw them into the van …

– P297, *Local girl, Fourth class, School 6*

Children also reported incidents of migrant aggression which involved them personally. The following two examples are from the same school and both involve an area close to the school:

Local girl 1: I don't like the Kelly Road.

Local girl 2: Oh no, it's very scary like ...

Inter: What's going on there?

Local girl 2: ... all the foreign people go around and they all chase you ...

Inter: Oh do they?

Local girl 2: ... and they're all shouting [argh] across from each other like when we're walking past and it's very scary.

Inter: And would that happen like a lot of the time?

Local girl 2: And when we're going up to the Alexander Park, we only went up yesterday ...

Local girl 1: And like you're only walking and they chase you with frying pans and all ...

Inter: Really?

Local girl 1: 'Hey you, what you doing?' [argh] [*laughter*].

– P151/277, Local girls, Fifth class, School 7

Local girl 2: ... yeah, and they were black, and I was walking down and like there does be like a load of blackies like on the Kelly Road ...

Inter: Yeah.

Local girl 1: ... and I was walking down with me friend from the park because me Ma left me there and I was going up to me Nanny's and they were chasing a rat around, right? And they picked the rat up and they goes 'you want to get in the car, get in the car' to me, and me friend was there like, 'cause I was on the inside and she was on two skates, and here they are 'you get in the car' but I legged it I did.

– P78/274, Local girls, Fifth class, School 7

As a footnote on the subject of beliefs about adult foreign nationals in Ireland, it is worth mentioning that a small number of children at School 6 reported an unusual belief that the world will end if there is a black pope:

> Everybody says when there is a black pope the world is going to end.
>
> – P4, Local girl, Fourth class, School 6

> And if we have a coloured president, no pope then the world will end.
>
> – P62, Local girl, Fifth class, School 6

As well as negative beliefs about migrant adults, children also expressed a range of opinions which were far more emotive, basically reflecting very negative feelings towards adult migrants to Ireland. This could vary from a fairly jingoistic catchphrase which gets a laugh from peers (e.g. '… they should be in their own country' – P164, Sixth class, School 6) to the more passionate emotional reaction in the following extract which is given at length because of its unusual violence:

> *Inter*: Okay, back to the question because we were talking about do you think it's a good thing to have people from different countries in your school?
>
> *Local girl 1*: No.
>
> *Inter*: No yeah? And what makes it difficult?
>
> *Local girl 1*: They do be like, you know they're talking about you, because they do be pointing at you and laughing. And like if you say anything to them they go up and tell the teacher and I can't even say hey to them because they go up and tell the teacher.
>
> *Local girl 2*: Because just say like you know Ania or Berta, she throws a basketball at you and hits you, and I went

Social Interaction 3: Prejudice, Bullying and Their Consequences

up to tell the teacher. Her and Dede were fighting one time in the yard. Dede's Ma came in and was kicking everybody's door in.

Inter: Do you think, what do you think they could do differently for it to be better?

Local girl 1: Get them out.

Inter: Yeah.

Local girl 1: Just have an all Irish school.

Inter: An all Irish school? That would be better? Yeah?

Local girl 1: Yeah because like if they want to go to school, they can go back over to their own country, we're not stopping them.

Inter: Yeah okay?

Local girl 1: And why are they even all moving over to this country? I don't like that because it's too dangerous with them all over here.

Inter: Ok yeah. And …

Local girl 1: Because like I live beside these flats and everybody calls them the [*inaudible*] and they have loads of shirts and they do all end up in my wall and I do be terrified and like they do keep me awake and I don't even find myself going asleep.

Inter: Okay and so, so you don't think that people from different countries get along well in your school do you? No okay.

Local girl 1: Kick them all out.

Inter: Do you think that people from different countries, you don't think that they get along well in your neighbourhood either?

Local girl 2: No, there's no one from different countries in my ...

Inter: No other people from different countries in your neighbourhood?

Local girl 2: I don't think there is anyway.

Local girl 1: Yes there is and they're always getting kicked up and down.

Inter: They're always getting kicked up and down? By who? Who's kicking them up and down?

Local girl 1: Everybody who hates them.

Inter: Who is it?

Local girl 1: Haven't even got a clue what their names are.

Inter: Do they live in your street? Yeah? And where are they from do you know?

Local girl 1: They live in Malone Road or something. They just disease me.

Inter: They just ...?

Local girl 1: Disease me.

Inter: They just disease you? Okay.

Local girl 1: Everybody diseases me that's from a different country.

– P62/30, *Local girls, Fifth class, School 6*

This is an extreme case. More common representations in this vein link migrants with dirt and/or unpleasant smelling food:

Local girl 1: ... these are blue flats, but like loads of foreign people live in them, like none Irish people live in them, and they do have like their legs hanging out the windows and all, it's horrible. And like their windows and all does be filthy and all and like they do have their

Social Interaction 3: Prejudice, Bullying and Their Consequences

blinds pulled across so you can see in. Like all the dirt in their house and all and like it's horrible.

Local girl 2: And like it's horrible they do have like chicken legs on strings and ... I don't know they probably don't have something to eat.

Local girl 1: And they've all clothes hanging out their windows and all, it's horrible.

– P44/76, *Local girls, Fifth class, School 6*

Many of the beliefs and attitudes reviewed above have a distinctly adult ring, a specific form and content which are not directly related to the child's social world. For reasons to do with ethical approval, we did not ask children directly about the sources of their attitudes. However, sources were sometimes identified spontaneously by children, the most common being parents:

Local girl: Oh Indian people I think they're scary.

Inter: Yeah, scary?

Local girl: My Ma's afraid that they'll touch me.

– P274, *Local girl, Fifth class, School 7*

Local girl 1: But some people from different countries they are like totally mean because my Da's friend owns a lock-up ...

Inter: They are totally what?

Local girl 2: Mean.

Local girl 1: ... like some people – maybe not totally mean – but some of them, like most of them are really nice but there's – I think they're all from Poland because my Da's friend owns a lock-up but like it's a gateway but the gate joins two different – a garage and a lock-up ...

Inter: Okay.

> *Local girl 1*: … and I don't know what a lock-up is but me Da's friend owns it.
>
> *Inter*: Okay.
>
> *Local girl 1*: But they won't move the cars or anything so it's blocking the lock-up so my Da's friend can't get into it, like he can get in but he can't bring a van or a car in.
>
> – P56/293, Local girls, Fifth class, School 6
>
> *Local boy 1*: There is one of them up – it's horrible there is a thing up in Yeats Street I don't know where it actually is but me dad was telling me.
>
> *Local boy 2*: Yeats Street? I don't know where Yeats Street is.
>
> *Local boy 1*: Oh yeah and they sell – they have a dog in the like they have a dog that they can eat in the front window.
>
> – P98/175, Local boys, Sixth class, School 2

Many children reported that inter-ethnic relations in their neighbourhood were difficult and some reported detailed accounts of assaults or other forms of abuse they had witnessed. Again, although it was not unique to this school, a large number of these accounts were to be found among children at School 6. Here are five representative examples, four of which come from School 6:

> … when anybody who walks by, and you know what, this man, this man right, he's from a different nationality he was just walking, he was just on his bike right, you know a motorbike, and he was just like and he was just going along and this man said 'can I have a shot on your bike for two minutes?', and he said 'no I've got to go somewhere very quickly' and then they

dragged him off the bike, they battered him, and even berserk right, and then they robbed his bike and all ...

– *P297, Local girl, Fourth class, School 6*

Like some people hate foreigners like they – they like kill Chinese people down my way sometimes. That's the only thing I don't like about it. Like some boys they get locked up an all cause they – a Chinese man like was ordering a pizza or delivering a pizza and um he got like people killed him – like not like kill like die like he was battered ...

– *P179, Local girl, Fourth class, School 6*

Inter: Do you think that people from different countries get on well in your area?

Local girl 1: Yeah sometimes really but not really like ...

Inter: Why not?

Local girl 1: ... other people can be calling them names and calling them like different colours and all.

Local girl 2: Call them something that we're not allowed say in the school.

Local girl 1: And they can't play or they can't do anything like. And like they always say 'no you're not playing, get away' and all.

– *P205/273, Local girls, Fourth class, School 6*

Inter: Okay. What do you think about people coming from all over the world to live in Ireland?

Local girl: Some of them take over. All our town is called – well it's not – all our town is full of Chinese and people call it Chinatown ...

Inter: Okay.

Local girl: ... because all of the Chinese there is in town.

Inter: And do you think that the Chinese people generally get on well in your area?

Local girl: Well some of them don't like, they get killed for nothing by the boys outside me door.

Inter: Okay.

Local girl: And all Polish people as well.

– P323, Local girl, Fourth class, School 6

Inter: What's the main big changes you can see?

Local girl: Well there's people from different countries coming over, they're different colours like – there's nothing wrong with that but then again you see people slagging them and all.

Inter: Yeah.

Local girl: So it's hard on them but.

– P308, Local girl, Fifth class, School 7

Reports such as these may also help to explain to some extent the experiences of School 6. In a study such as this, it was difficult to explore deeply the reasons why this school experienced such problems in relation to the attitudes of its pupils. We can say that, on the surface, we could observe nothing unusual about the school itself. The principal and teachers appeared warm and competent. Although we would emphatically state that we cannot answer the question why, we can offer a suggestion which we think would be worth following up. Based on the unusual amount of racial aggression which children at the school reported witnessing, and the fact that some children reported hearing negative stories about migrants from parents, we would suggest that one of the reasons that this school was experiencing such difficulties may have been because of particular problems in the community which the school served.

Prejudice towards Other Children: Ethnic Name-Calling and Racial Bullying

When we consider bullying we must bear in mind that schools can sometimes be rough places for all children and that the schools in which we worked were located in traditionally working class neighbourhoods where life can at times involve both playful and more harmful forms of physical interaction. Local children can themselves be the targets of quite vicious victimisation. For example, the girl referred to in the following account has been identified as Irish and other children in the class reported corroborating observations:

> But there's this one girl in our class and like nobody treats her – like everybody treats her different as if she's not like – as if she's not a human but if we – like I would feel sorry for her because nobody plays with her or anything.
>
> – P56, Local girl, Fifth class, School 6

Throughout our interviews, there are frequent accounts of fights, name-calling and bullying. These may have little or nothing to do with race or ethnicity even when they involve migrant children. One Russian girl explains:

> *Inter*: So like and do people ever like say bad things or anything like that?
>
> *Russian girl*: Not like maybe exactly really, no just like the way they would …
>
> *Inter*: Yeah.
>
> *Russian girl*: … say it to anyone really so.
>
> – P322, Russian girl, Fifth class, School 7

However, there are also numerous incidents which have specifically racial overtones, or which appear to have. The use of ethnic slurs to refer to migrant children occurs both in and out of school, although there does seem to be a reluctance to talk about it on all sides. The most common way in which we heard about it was at second-hand, one child reporting what another said to another:

> Like I saw this before when a girl called Rudo and people call her chocolate bar cos she's black.
>
> – P218, Local girl, Sixth class, School 1

> Yeah. Sometimes – once she [girl in the class] called them [three Indian girls in the class] a Paki, remember?
>
> – P308, Local girl, Fifth class, School 7

> *Local girl*: Karl keeps on saying to Jenny, it's a bad word, I can't say it in school.
>
> *Inter*: You can say it here, I won't tell anybody you said it.
>
> *Local girl*: He says to her she's a fucking foreigner.
>
> – P221, Local girl, Sixth class, School 6

Many migrant children were reluctant to talk about details but simply reported that other children had been mean to them or called them names. Some children provide more detail about the kinds of taunts they receive:

> The boys in my class said I'm made from Poo.
>
> – P270, Nigerian girl, First class, School 5

> Some people would say it's not good Pakistan.
>
> – P317, Pakistani girl, Fifth class, School 7

> *Local girl*: … some people may be like, might be a bit mean.

> *Inter*: Okay.
>
> *Russian girl*: Yeah. Like somebody might try to copy and repeat how I talk.
>
> *Inter*: Okay.
>
> *Local girl*: Yeah they'd be like copying – mimic the way they speak or something.
>
> *– P322/14, Russian and local girls, Fifth class, School 7*

A strong sense that it is bad to engage in ethnic name-calling came across in the interviews:

> You don't slag them [people who are 'half-cast'].
>
> *– P142, Local girl, Fourth class, School 3*

Some children believe that there can be a certain coolness attached to using ethnic names abusively (probably related to the fact that they are considered 'bad'):

> I think they just want to be cool. Just 'cos they want to show off in front of their friends.
>
> *– P218, Local girl, Sixth class, School 1*

Related to the sense that ethnic name-calling is a bad thing is a less frequent phenomenon, in which some children say that they only use these terms in retaliation:

> … me or my friends only call the Chinese people Chinky when they call us Paddys.
>
> *– P150, Local boy, Second class, School 2*

More persistent bullying on the basis of nationality also emerged as an issue.

> *Inter*: Okay, has anybody ever been mean to you in school?

Hungarian girl: Sometimes.

Inter: Yeah what happens when somebody is mean to you in school?

Hungarian girl: They're like talking and they're like thinking that you're ... they're from Ireland or they're here for a long time.

– P111, Hungarian girl, Sixth class, School 6

Slovenian girl: I don't know I feel like stupid because of no English I think and always seem like, it was not good for me, and always when I came back home I was crying that they were ...

Inter: Oh no.

Slovenian girl: ... punching me or something. I was like feeling very bad.

Inter: You were very upset by it, were you? And were these girls in your class?

Slovenian girl: Yeah.

– P31, Slovenian girl, Fifth class, School 7

Two girls in the same class describe in more detail the kind of interaction that goes on and offer an explanation why migrant children do not report what is happening:

Inter: Okay, so do you think then some people, are they a bit rough on people from different countries ...

Local girl 1: Yeah.

Inter: ... would you say? Yeah? In what way would they be like?

Local girl 1: Just like – they wouldn't hit them or nothing ...

Inter: Yeah.

Local girl 1: ... just the eyes and 'what you're looking at?'

Local girl 2: They giving them the looks and all ...

Inter: Okay.

Local girl 2: ... and saying 'What you looking at?'

Local girl 1: But like they'd be ...

Local girl 2: 'Go back to your own country.'

Inter: Yeah.

Local girl 1: ...yeah and all but they wouldn't stick up for themselves, you know, the girls from different countries ...

Inter: Yeah.

Local girl 1: ... they'd be too afraid to so it's hard for them like.

Inter: Do you think like do they not understand, like the way that like people go on or what do you think?

Local girl 1: They kind of do ...

Inter: Yeah.

Local girl 1: ... but like they'd just be a bit scared to like ...

Inter: Yeah.

Local girl 2: Yeah.

Local girl 1: ... they don't know what's going to happen to them or anything.

– P308/235, *Local girls, Fifth class, School 7*

The account of a migrant child in a different school supports this explanation of why children are reluctant to seek help:

Nigerian boy: They always call me names.

Inter: Okay. Do they hurt your feelings, do they? Ah, and why do you think they do that?

Nigerian boy: I don't know why.

Inter: You don't know why. And do you ever tell the teacher or your Mam or anything? No. And why don't you tell them?

Nigerian boy: Because if I tell on them and they get in trouble they will start to ...

Inter: Okay.

Nigerian boy: ... then they'll run away and hide some place.

Inter: Okay. So you don't think anything is going to happen even if you say something, [*Shakes head*] no? And are people mean to people if they tell, are they? [*Shakes head*] What do they say if you – if people tell?

Nigerian boy: They will call me names after you tell on them.

– P268, Nigerian boy, School 2

Although migrant children from many different countries report being bullied or isolated, skin colour is a very important dimension of such behaviour:

Inter: Ok, do you remember what your first day at this school was like?

Romanian girl: Yeah it was really fun but we miss our old teacher don't we?

Nigerian girl: But I didn't have any fun because everyone was bullying me, that's because I was brown.

– P321/270, Romanian and Nigerian girls, First class, School 5

Inter: Are any people mean or slag you or any of that kind of thing?

Nigerian boy: Sometimes.

Social Interaction 3: Prejudice, Bullying and Their Consequences

Inter: And what would they be saying?

Nigerian boy: Sometimes they say that I am not from Ireland but I am.

Inter: Yes, and why do you think they say you are not from Ireland?

Nigerian boy: Because my body is not white.

Inter: And do many people make a big deal out of that, do they?

Nigerian boy: Yes.

– P339, *Nigerian boy, Second class, School 2*

Many cases of bullying can be difficult to classify in terms of whether race is involved as an issue or not. For instance, in the following example, we may have our suspicions but it is genuinely hard to tell:

Inter: Okay, has anybody ever been mean to you in school?

Nigerian boy: Yes, when I started... actually when I started everybody was good to me but after about one month or two they started being mean and things like that.

Inter: How were they mean to you?

Nigerian boy: They didn't let me play any games with them and I think they called me ... well they said things about me behind my back, things like that.

– P171, *Nigerian boy, Sixth class, School 2*

In this case, the interview did not throw any further light on the reasons why the boy was picked on. A similar account was given at the start of a different interview:

Inter: And is anyone ever mean to you in class?

> *Nigerian boy*: Yes.
>
> *Inter*: Who is mean to you?
>
> *Nigerian boy*: Michael is mean to me.
>
> *Inter*: And why is he mean to you?
>
> *Nigerian boy*: Because ... I forget.
>
> *Inter*: Does he ever say anything to you?
>
> *Nigerian boy*: No but he keeps whacking your head with a book.
>
> – P171, Nigerian boy, Second class, School 2

However, in this case the subject arose again at a later stage of the interview and it appeared quite clearly that ethnicity was involved:

> *Inter*: Why would they laugh at you?
>
> *Nigerian boy*: Because they called me black.
>
> *Inter*: Did they, right, and how does that make you feel?
>
> *Nigerian boy*: Sad.
>
> *Inter*: And who says that to you?
>
> *Nigerian boy*: Michael.
>
> *Inter*: And why do you think he says that?
>
> *Nigerian boy*: Just because I am brown.
>
> – P171, Nigerian boy, Second class, School 2

In light of this example, the genuine ambiguity of the previous case becomes apparent. This example is also important in reminding us of the difficulties we face when trying to access children's experiences of racism.

A small number of migrant children also seem to be bullied by secondary school children on the way home from school:

Local boy 1: But one boy got bullied the first day he came into school.

Inter: Yeah?

Local boy 1: Smashed him.

Local boy 2: By who?

Local boy 1: By a boy that's in secondary school.

Inter: Yeah?

Local boy 3: Who?

Local boy 2: I didn't know that.

Inter: What happened?

Local boy 1: He just started throwing stuff an all and slagging him.

– P98/169/175, Local boys, Sixth class, School 2

A Nigerian boy at the same school reported a similar experience:

Nigerian boy: Yeah, like I got chased one day by the secondary boys and they walked right into my gate.

Inter: By secondary school boys, did you? And would secondary school boys say things a lot?

Nigerian boy: Yeah and they laugh at me.

– P268, Nigerian boy, Second class, School 2

Finally, we should also bear in mind that bullying is not exclusively by local children and directed at migrant children. In the following extract two children give their perspective on a situation in their class in which a Romanian child who appears to be having difficulties with some local children picks on another Romanian child:

Mongolian boy: The only way that Michael and all the boys annoy Alexandru is because Alexandru annoys him and he doesn't really like that.

Local boy: The teachers think that they are bullying him but sometimes he does bring it on himself.

Inter: And what would he do to bring it on himself?

Local boy: If somebody kicked the ball and hit him in the back he'd turn around, he wouldn't know much English but he'd turn around and shout, what are you doing that for?

Inter: Ok.

Mongolian boy: He usually picks on Anton.

Inter: He picks on Anton, and Anton is new as well. And why do you think he picks on Anton?

Mongolian boy: Because he is afraid to go to us.

Local boy: He is afraid to hit anybody else or bully anybody else so he bullies Anton because he knows Anton is weak because he doesn't know much English.

– *P327/168, Mongolian and local boys, Sixth class, School 1*

The Consequences of Ethnic Bullying

A growing body of international research tells us that children who are exposed to racism can experience a wide variety of negative symptoms as a result. We will discuss this literature at the end of this chapter. For now, we can note that perceived racism by children has been associated with negative mental health outcomes such as depression and low self-esteem, as well as different forms of hostility directed outwards at others. The following section gives a flavour of children's experiences of racism and their responses to it.

In some cases, children who had experienced racial bullying talked about how they looked forward to leaving Ireland:

Inter: Okay, so in Ireland here, do you feel the same or different to people in Ireland?

Polish girl: Different.

Inter: Different?

Both girls: Yes.

Inter: Which way exactly do you feel different?

Polish girl: The way that when I come to school the ...

Slovenian girl: It's the same talking.

Polish girl: ... that hurt me and that I don't want to like – if I be, come again to Ireland I don't want to.

Inter: You don't want to come again?

Polish girl: Yeah.

Inter: Okay. So you kind of – you feel that you've been treated kind of badly, do you?

Polish girl: Yeah.

Inter: Yeah, okay. So what do you think – are you going to go back to Poland then?

Polish girl: Yeah.

Inter: Yeah.

Polish girl: I think in sixth class I will go to Poland.

– *P317/267, Slovenian and Polish girls, Fifth class, School 7*

Other children expressed more intense anger and resentment towards the local children who bullied them. The following account concerns a multi-racial local girl:

Local girl 1: Just giving us the looks and saying 'What you looking at?' and 'Why are you getting interfered and all with?'

Inter: Yeah and like how does it make you feel when they'd be doing all that sort of stuff?

Local girl 1: Just I wish I could get all me anger out but like I just ...

Local girl 2: You would be afraid sometimes, wouldn't you?

Local girl 1: ... yeah.

Inter: Yeah.

Local girl 2: Like we don't let them do it to us now 'cause like we're older.

Local girl 1: But they won't hit us or anything they just say stuff to us.

– P235/308, Slovenian and Polish girls, Fifth class, School 7

In the following extract, two friends talk about very different strategies they adopt for dealing with girls who pick on them:

Inter: What happens when people are mean to you in school?

Polish girl: They start to get mean to ye and then you like, just can't manage it and then you start to get bitchy back and then there's all rows.

Malaysian girl: I don't really react kind of.

Polish girl: She kind of ignores it. I don't know how she does it!

Inter: Yeah, it's probably a really good strategy, not to react.

Malaysian girl: Just ignored it.

Polish girl: I can't.

Malaysian girl: Block your ears and then you can't hear them.

– P91/281, Polish and Malaysian girls, Fifth class, School 6

As with the Malaysian girl in this extract, some children appear to suffer bullying and racism much more passively than others.

> *Inter*: And it hits ye? ... and how does that make ye feel then when they shoutin' at ye and all that sort of stuff?
>
> *Romanian boy*: Not good, like.
>
> *Inter*: Yeah?
>
> *Romanian boy*: Like, I've been ... be sad an all.
>
> – P136, Romanian boy, Second class, School 2

In the interview from which the following extract is taken, the eight-year-old boy often found it hard to articulate his feelings, but the overall impression is that he was quite overwhelmed by his experiences. He has just been talking not only about the fact that he is bad at football, but also about the fact that he has been the victim of some quite serious racial abuse:

> *Nigerian boy*: People think I'm bad.
>
> *Inter*: How? [*Pause.*] Why do they think you're bad? [*Boy shakes head.*] You don't know? And how does that make you feel when they're saying that? Ah. [*Boy starts to cry. Interview stopped.*]
>
> – P268, Nigerian boy, Second class, School 2

Isolation and bullying can also have a predictable impact on self-esteem:

> *Inter*: In what way do you feel a bit different? Just in your area where you live.
>
> *Nigerian boy*: Because there are not lots of people that like me so that is why I try and make friends.
>
> *Inter*: Okay, so how do you feel about that?
>
> *Nigerian boy*: I feel a bit sad.

Inter: Okay, and why don't you think that they like you?

Nigerian boy: Because I don't know much about everything.

– P339, Nigerian boy, Second class, School 2

The most serious and distressing consequence of racial bullying which we encountered was among black children who had reached the point of wishing to change their skin colour.

Inter: Why are you different?

Nigerian girl: Because everybody is white and I'm brown.

Inter: Okay. So what do you think – but is there any other way that you're different?

Nigerian girl: No.

Inter: No. So is there anyone else who is brown in your class?

Nigerian girl: Yeah.

Inter: Yeah.

Nigerian girl: Ellen.

Inter: Ellen is, yeah.

Nigerian girl: And and Aaron.

Inter: Aaron yeah.

Nigerian girl: That's all.

Inter: That's all, yeah. And so are there any other girls that you play with in the yard who are brown?

Nigerian Girl: I play with Belle and Pearl.

Inter: Okay, lovely. And is there any – so what do you think, is it good or is it bad to be different?

Nigerian girl: Bad.

Inter: Why is it bad?

Nigerian girl: Because I don't like my skin.

Inter: Okay. And – I think your skin is lovely, it's beautiful. But why don't you like your skin?

Nigerian girl: Because it's brown.

– P342, Nigerian girl, Senior Infants class, School 7

Nigerian boy: I am the smartest in the class.

Inter: You are, you are very smart, I saw that yes. What subjects do you like the best?

Nigerian boy: Science and Maths.

Inter: That's good. And who else is smart in your class?

Nigerian boy: Simon is not very smart.

Inter: But are you smarter than Simon?

Nigerian boy: Yes.

Inter: Who else are you smarter than?

Nigerian boy: Sally.

Inter: So you are good at that. So if you could change anything about yourself, would you change anything?

Nigerian boy: Yes.

Inter: What would you change?

Nigerian boy: My body.

Inter: You'd change your body, in what way?

Nigerian boy: I'd turn into white.

Inter: You'd turn into white, why would you do that?

Nigerian boy: So people can't laugh at me.

Inter: Why would they laugh at you?

Nigerian boy: Because they called me black.

Inter: Did they, right, and how does that make you feel?

Nigerian boy: Sad.

Inter: And who says that to you?

Nigerian boy: Michael.

Inter: And why do you think he says that?

Nigerian boy: Just because I am brown.

Inter: But do you think it is a very nice thing to do?

Nigerian boy: No.

Inter: And have you ever told your mam or anything about that?

Nigerian boy: Yes.

Inter: And what does she say?

Nigerian boy: She said that she would tell their ma that they are doing it.

Inter: And did they say it to anyone else in your class?

Nigerian boy: No.

Inter: And how long have they been saying those things?

Nigerian boy: Since senior infants.

Inter: And does it hurt your feelings?

Nigerian boy: Yes.

Inter: What do you think you are better than them at?

Nigerian boy: Writing.

– P171, Nigerian boy, Second class, School 1

Discussion

The term 'ethnocentric' was introduced over 100 years ago (Sumner, 1906) and refers to a tendency to perceive your own group as central and to measure all other groups relative to it. Since then, ethnocentrism has been extensively studied and been found to be pervasive across human cultures (see Segall at al., 1999). Different cultural perspectives have evolved different ethnocentric belief systems. The type of ethnocentrism encountered in this research which represents non-western countries as war-torn, famished, and backward is quite widespread and is part of a broader outlook known as *Eurocentrism* (Amin, 1988). As we discussed in Chapter 2, migrants into Ireland in the last 15 years have been a relatively highly skilled, highly educated group. In Chapter 5, we have seen that this is often reflected in the children of migrants who are typically reported as hard-working, studious and well-behaved. The power of ethnocentric, stereotypical beliefs is clearly demonstrated in the persistence of such beliefs among even very young children and among children who are in regular contact with migrant children who confound those stereotypes. Such stereotypes form an important backdrop for interaction between local and migrant children in the inner-city and their widespread prevalence should not blind us to their potential harmful consequences. Such stereotypes can distort perceptions and colour relationships before they begin, suggesting, at best, a tone of paternalism and pity, at worst one of condescension and revulsion.

The local children in our study were definitely aware of the changes that migration had brought to their communities. While many children had positive or indifferent attitudes to these changes, some children had quite negative views of the impact of migration. Smyth, Darmody, McGinnity and Byrne (2009) found evidence of similar concerns among children in their focus group study. In the present study, School 6 was unusual in that many pupils in the school expressed quite intense resentment of adult migrants and were likely to report that they had witnessed assaults upon migrants. As we said, the reasons why this school stood out in this way are at present unclear, but we think the finding is important from a number of perspectives. Firstly, it tells us that the experience of schools can vary quite dramatically and that we must be very careful in generalising from one school context to another. Schools in even very close proximity can be quite different. School staff generally seem to be unaware of this fact. Secondly, from a policy point of view, it is important to take on board that some schools and areas may face far more intense challenges in relation to the integration of children than others. We will return to this issue in the final chapter. As we might expect, racial bullying was also a serious issue in this school. However, we have also seen that racial bullying of equal intensity occurred in the other schools. On this basis, we might speculate that negative attitudes towards adult migrants may be related to racial bullying, but that racial bullying may also occur in the absence of such attitudes. Quantitative research is needed to determine the precise nature of the relationship between negative attitudes towards migrants and racial bullying in schools. For now, we believe the following hypothesis is reasonable: children who are prejudiced against migrants will be more likely to engage in racial bullying, but racial bullying may also occur simply in the context of ethnocentric beliefs about foreigners and as a direct reaction to perceived difference.

The present research also found that racial bullying was quite common in these primary schools in the inner-city and that it could be quite intense. Three Irish studies, which we reviewed in Chapter 2, offer different perspectives on the existence and prevalence of racial bullying. A survey by Smyth, McCoy and Darmody (2004) found that a greater proportion of non-national, than Irish, students had experienced bullying, in particular being 'Jeered', 'Upset by things said', 'Ignored' and 'Physically pushed'. Devine and Kelly (2002) in their qualitative study of three primary schools found that both minority and majority children did not identify racism and/or hostile attitudes to minority ethnic children as a major problem in school, but that minority children of all ages recounted instances of racist abuse in their out-of-school lives. The researchers also found that children considered name-calling in relation to skin colour 'mean'. The present research also found that children generally expressed disapproval of ethnic name-calling. However, we also found that such name-calling along with more aggressive forms of ethnic bullying took place both inside and outside of school. The difference between the present work and that of Devine and Kelly (2002) may be explained by one or all of the following:

- Individual schools appear to differ in incidence and intensity of ethnic bullying.

- Methodological differences: In our research we found that the most distressing accounts of bullying were reported in one-to-one interviews with migrant children. Devine and Kelly (2002) used larger group interviews.

- The time interval between the two studies.

In their national survey of school principals, Smyth, Darmody, McGinnity and Byrne (2009) found that 8 per cent of school principals believed that bullying and racism contributed 'A lot' or 'Quite a lot' to difficulties among newcomer students. As we discussed in Chapter 4, we believe that the perspectives of adults on issues to do with the child's social world must be treated with circumspection, a view also echoed by the authors of the survey of principals. In their qualitative research with children, Smyth, Darmody, McGinnity and Byrne (2009) also found that some newcomer children had experienced bullying on the grounds of nationality or ethnicity and, like Devine and Kelly (2002), found that students in the two working class schools they visited distinguished between an absence of racism in the school and the reality of racist behaviour in the local neighbourhood. In the present study, we found that intense racism could occur within the school environment, a difference which may again be explained by differences between school contexts and methodological approaches (the methodology of the Smyth,

Darmody, McGinnity and Byrne (2009) study involved focus groups). Considering the reluctance of some children to report details of racist incidents which we discussed in this chapter, focus groups may not fully penetrate the social life of the children taking part.

As an issue, racism has received a lot of attention, both in the media and among researchers. This can mean that people can begin to take it for granted despite its pernicious nature. When presenting evidence of racism to researchers and other adults, the authors have sometimes met an attitude of 'It's only racism, we know about that'. However, if we look at the accounts of racism given by children themselves, we come away with a sense that for them, this is not something familiar and taken for granted. It can be very raw, upsetting and unexpected, something they struggle to make sense of. Often, they seem to get little help to do so.

Finally, we note that racism has consequences beyond the unpleasant, hurtful, immediate experience. In a review of international research on the link between childhood experience of racism and physical and mental health outcomes, Pachter and Coll (2009) found that children's experience of racism has been linked to depression, anxiety, low self-esteem, conduct problems including delinquency and substance use, and cardiovascular and metabolic disease. Some of the psychological consequences of racism can already be seen emerging among some of the children we spoke to, in particular resentment and low self-esteem. The finding that a number of children are experiencing severe remorse over their skin colour is perhaps one of the most important findings from the present research. Even if the numbers are small, the implications are very serious. Such children represent the worst victims of racial bullying, the most salient cases of an underlying problem. These children are good, hard-working pupils, loyal and earnest. The consequences of the victimisation that they suffer will likely be with them the rest of their lives. Any attempt to minimise or dismiss their experience should be challenged very strongly.

Chapter 8

Where To from Here? Policy Challenges

In this chapter, we assess possible policy responses that can be made to offset the kinds of ethnic distance and hostility among children that we encountered in this study. What can we do to ensure that future generations of children in Ireland do not encounter the same problems and get the most from growing up in multi-cultural schools and communities? We argue that there is no simple answer to this question; rather, what is vital at this point in time is a commitment to a realistic process for finding answers.

Although this research did find positive interaction between local and migrant children in Dublin's north inner-city primary schools, some serious divisions were also noted. The more common of these was a distance or 'separateness' in interaction between the two. A clear strand of racially motivated bullying was also identified. Internationally, difficulties in inter-ethnic relations have often been found to fester over time. In countries with a history of inter-ethnic conflict, simple de-segregation has been found to do little to improve relations (Brown and Hewstone, 2005; Pedersen, Walker, and Wise, 2005; Schofield and Eurich-Fulcer, 2003). As a rule, passivity tends to be associated with deterioration rather than amelioration. It therefore seems likely that the passage of time will bring deeper separation and ethnic tension. As attitudes become more deeply entrenched and a history of distance and problems accumulates, the issues will become more difficult to address. We believe the current situation is one which requires urgent attention. However, we immediately encounter another problem: what should be done? The answer is far from obvious. As we will see, the kinds of possible solutions which can be suggested are not perfect and even if we could bring together an ideal package of best available practice implementation presents an enormous challenge.

In this chapter, we outline an approach to enhancing inter-ethnic relations in Irish schools that we believe is feasible and evidence-based. We will present our argument under the following headings:

1. Reasonable aims for social integration policy in relation to children
2. What needs to be done?
3. Existing policy and practice in Ireland
4. Possibilities of implementing new policies and practices in Ireland.

Reasonable Aims for Social Integration Policy in Relation to Children

The more specific we can be about our aims, the more focused we can be in our search for answers. On the basis of the research we reviewed for this book, we believe that the following are all legitimate and immediately relevant goals for integration policy in Ireland as it relates to children:

- To provide all children with a common language with which they can communicate with one another
- To encourage children of different cultural backgrounds to interact freely and get to know one another
- To reduce racial bullying and name calling as far as possible
- To discourage children from holding ethnocentric and prejudicial beliefs

Where To from Here? Policy Challenges

- To encourage children to be knowledgeable about other countries and cultures
- To discourage adults from communicating prejudiced beliefs to children and young people.

This is a very short and, in some ways, a very simple list. Other commentators would wish to add to it. However, it is already a tall order. We believe this list best reflects what is required to promote positive inter-ethnic relations among the current generation of children in Ireland.

Of course, there can be no suggestion of forcing children to get along or mix. The aim is to create a free environment in which children are open to mixing, where it seems the 'natural' and 'logical' thing to do. We are hoping to foster a climate where children will feel motivated to approach other children with as little pre-judgement ('prejudice') as possible. This is a formidable challenge: we are trying to influence interaction deep inside the social world of children. We are trying to ensure that this happens consistently across the country. Obviously, the first two aims relate to those schools which have numbers of minority children while the last two are relevant to all schools.

What Needs to Be Done?

In order to make progress in achieving these aims, we believe it is helpful to think in terms of two broad spaces we need to influence: an adult world and a child's world. The distinction is in some ways obvious but it does flow from our findings. It also has important ramifications for how we think about the kinds of action we need to take.

Within the adult world, achieving change requires creating a willingness to consider, promote and implement reform in this area. This will involve the enormous task of raising awareness and gaining recognition of both the importance of active integration and the prevalence and seriousness of racial hostility among children. It is important that both educators and policy makers gain a deeper understanding of these issues. Individual schools and NGOs have made remarkable and laudable attempts to promote diversity and discourage racism among children. These efforts should be valued, encouraged and expanded. Added to this we need high quality, evidence-based, multimedia efforts to present relevant information to educators, policy makers and parents and to engage with them around these issues. Key messages are the value of cross-cultural engagement as opposed to separateness, the tendency of racism targeted at children often to remain hidden within the child's social world, research evidence on the actual experience of bullying and racism and the physical and psychological consequences of racism. Adult support is fundamental for successful implementation of any initiative to enhance inter-ethnic relations among children.

There is no getting around the fact that schools and teachers have a particularly important role to play in ensuring social cohesion within the child's social world in multi-cultural communities. The broader community also has an important role to play. Schools are of course the site in which migrant and local children have their most active and extensive exposure to each other. The traditions of intervention which have the greatest history of success (reviewed below) are all school-based and involve quite profound changes to teaching practice and content. Even if we only attempt to build on the existing curriculum – which will probably have limited effectiveness – we are talking about quite large additions to teaching materials. The forces operating against change are powerful. Schools and teachers already have established routines. Schools which have to meet the other challenges which migration brings are often heavily preoccupied with just teaching the curriculum. The locations in which intervention is needed most are often facing many other challenges through social disadvantage – in some cases, children may be in more urgent need of a social worker than a social or educational psychologist. In such situations, cultural differences are often layered with other differences in social experience and outlook. In addition, the adult community itself may be hostile to integration. There is virtually no information on how existing forms of intervention deal with such situations. In addition to that, the social life of children in schools may be so arranged (see discussion in Chapter 4) that teachers may not see many problems that arise. So the very people who are being asked to make substantial changes to their work practice may not see the need for any change at all. All in all, a huge amount of work needs to be done to influence the views of adults and, in particular, educators.

But it is within the child's social world, both inside and outside school, that we must produce change if we are to have deep engagement and credible progress towards our stated aims. This is no simple task. We are seeking to produce significant change in a world which is, for the most part, beyond adult surveillance. Genuine adult support is vital for this to succeed, but we then need to think very seriously about how it is that we can affect the social attitudes and practices of children. In the following section, we will review a range of approaches that have been used specifically with children. We will then consider how we might initiate a process for developing detailed and concrete packages for dealing with diversity among Irish school children – packages which are evidence-based, proven to work and feasible to implement.

Internationally, there has been an enormous number of experiments, initiatives and policies directed at enhancing inter-ethnic relations. In order to simplify our task, we are going to focus on those traditions which have a clear record of improving inter-ethnic relations among school children in high quality research tests. Research evidence is important. Inter-ethnic relations are notoriously difficult to influence and initiatives to improve them can have unintended, even unhelpful, consequences. Given that theoretically-driven, evidence-based initiatives have often met with mixed results, reliance on home-grown efforts at school, local or even national level is probably unwarranted (at the very least, until rigorous evaluation has taken place).

In relation to reducing prejudice and distance between children of different ethnic groups, three traditions stand out: *cooperative learning*, *multi-cultural curricula* and *social–cognitive skills training*. We will explain what each of these involves below. There are other new and exciting approaches, but extensive evidence is simply not yet available to permit an assessment of their effectiveness. Given the inevitably constrained resources which relevant Irish government agencies and NGOs have to devote to these issues, focusing on well-established traditions seems the best approach (at least in the near future, in terms of national policy).

To date, the single most influential approach to enhancing intergroup and inter-ethnic relationships is the 'contact hypothesis' (Allport, 1954). It predicts that contact between different groups will lead to a reduction in prejudice, provided certain conditions are met. The principal conditions are that group members should work together:

- Towards a common goal
- With interdependent roles
- With equal status
- In the context of policies which endorse the contact.

A considerable amount of research evidence has supported the validity of the approach and of the conditions which it sets out (Binder et al., 2009; Paolini, Hewstone, Harwood, and Cairns, 2006; Pettigrew and Tropp, 2006; Wagner, Tropp, Finchinescu, and Tredoux, 2008). However, an obvious problem is how to routinely engineer situations which meet the conditions of contact specified above. In relation to children, cooperative learning comes very close to doing so.

Cooperative learning has developed in many forms and has many different names. An older name that is less frequently used, 'interdependent learning', may reveal more about its essential nature. Cooperative learning refers to small group teaching and learning strategies which actively seek to promote interdependence among group members such that 'each member of a team is responsible not only for learning what is taught but also for helping teammates learn' (Ryan, Reid, and Epstein, 2004). Pupils work with little direct teacher supervision (Deering, 1989, as cited by Cooper and Slavin, 2004) on carefully planned and monitored activities (Slavin and Cooper, 1999) in such a way that each participant can achieve his or her learning goal if, and only if, the other group members achieve theirs. Cooperative learning is distinguished from traditional group work by the interdependence of the group members (and, significantly, by the level of planning by teachers). The difference between cooperative learning and regular group work is important to emphasise – in fact, traditional group work is often used as a comparison group to demonstrate the effectiveness of cooperative learning!

Cooperative learning strategies have been shown to have positive effects on many learning outcomes such as:

- Achievement (Cohen et al., 1997; Cohen and Lotan, 1997; Slavin, 1995)

- Self-esteem (De Vries, Slavin, Fennessey, Edwards, and Lombardo, 1980; Johnson, Johnson, Tiffany, and Zaidman, 1983; Slavin, 1980; Stephen, 1978)

- Social competency (Cohen and Lotan, 1995; Ginsburg-Block, Rohrbeck, and Fantuzzo, 2006; Roseth, Johnson, and Johnson, 2008)

- Quality of the learning environment (Aronson and Osherow, 1980; Aronson and Patnoe, 1997; Blaney, Stephen, Rosenfield, Aronson, and Silkes,1977; Geffner, 1978, as cited by Aronson and Osherow, 1980).

Cooperative learning is often promoted as a strategy to achieve these outcomes; it is not inherently designed to reduce prejudice or improve inter-group attitudes (Mckown, 2005; Singh, 1991). However, when used in classrooms which involve different ethnic groups, cooperative learning techniques reproduce many of the conditions specified by the 'contact hypothesis' above. In numerous research studies, cooperative learning has been found to be effective in improving inter-ethnic relations in the classroom (McKown, 2005). We review a few of these studies below. These represent only a small sample of a much larger literature. Of the three broad traditions which we will review here, cooperative learning has received by far the most research attention (Paluck and Green, 2008) and by the early 1990s, 79 per cent of US elementary schools reported using it (Puma et. al., 1993).

The positive impact of cooperative learning strategies on intergroup relations among children has a long documented history (early examples include Cohen and Roper, 1972; Cohen, Lockheed, and Lohman, 1976; Ziegler, 1981; Johnson and Johnson, 1981; Slavin and Oickle, 1981; Sharan, Hertz-Lazarowitz, Bejarano, Raviv, Sharan, 1984).[1] A review by Johnson and Johnson (1989) found that cooperative learning was associated with greater intergroup friendships between majority and minority group members. A more recent review by Ginsburg-Block et al. (2006) of Peer Assistant Learning interventions (which include cooperative learning) found a positive impact on 'social outcomes' under which they include positive inter-ethnic attitudes. A review of 19 field experiments using eight different cooperative learning paradigms by Cooper and Slavin (2004) found generally positive effects on prejudice and discrimination among children in fourth to twelfth grades where the minority presence was between 10 per cent and 61 per cent. Teachers require training in order to use cooperative learning strategies, but once familiar with them they can use ready-made lesson plans as well as adapting existing ones. Cooperative learning strategies are thus appealing, in policy terms, as they are relatively cheap to implement, can be used with

---

[1] Curry, Gilligan and DeAmicis are currently conducting an up-to-date systematic review of the use of cooperative learning to enhance intergroup relations in schools. This project is being conducted in partnership with the international Campbell Collaboration and is funded by the Irish Research Council on Humanities and Social Sciences. For more information, see the 'More about our project' section at the end of this book.

different ages and abilities and can be incorporated into existing school curricula (Singh, 1991; Slavin, 1995). Moreover, they can be presented to schools and educational policy makers as a means not only of improving inter-ethnic relations, but also as a way of improving a variety of more traditional 'academic' outcomes (McKown, 2005). Although much of the available evidence on cooperative learning comes from the US, testing the approach in Ireland seem like a worthwhile and feasible objective.

Irish primary schools are generally warm, cooperative and non-competitive. Compared to at least some countries, they may exude a more child-centred, less authoritarian atmosphere. They seem ideal for cooperative learning. However, it is not that simple. We will return to the profound challenges inherent in even limited use of cooperative learning in Irish primary schools in the final section of this chapter.

There is a long tradition internationally of using *multicultural curricula* to improve social relationships in multi-ethnic schools. According to Pfeifer et al. (2007), such approaches have involved either:

- Add-on modules which teach children about selected cultural groups and aim to challenge stereotypes, or
- Major revisions of entire curricula to reflect the diversity of the communities which schools serve.

The basic aim of multi-cultural curricula is to teach children a more realistic and positive understanding of other groups (Aboud and Levy, 2000). From the perspective of minority children, multicultural curricula may also serve an important function in terms of symbolising some kind of valuing of their cultural origin. In terms of impact on attitudes of majority children, evidence as to success of multi-cultural curricula has not been overwhelming. Some studies have demonstrated positive effects, but these effects have generally been weak. Other studies have found no effect (Levy et al., 2003). Part of this, however, may be due to design flaws in the research available. Very little is known about how multi-cultural curricula impact on ethnic victimisation (Bigler, 1999). However, even if we are cautious about the impact on the issues of concern in the previous section, multi-cultural curricula may still be regarded as having value. As Pfeifer, Spears-Brown and Juvonen (2007) put it so elegantly:

> Regardless of the effectiveness of multicultural curricula in reducing prejudice, there may be educational value in a multicultural education. At a minimum, it provides a more realistic, well-rounded context for learning necessary in our multicultural society.

Outside of the *relatively* coherent traditions represented by cooperative learning and multi-cultural curricula, there is a more nebulous group of approaches which in one way or another aim to change the way people think or feel about minority out-group members. One review refers to these as *social–cognitive skills training* (Pfeifer, Spears-Brown and Juvonen, 2007), while another considers them under the more basic descriptive labels of 'entertainment' and 'discussion and peer influence' (Paluck and Green, 2009). Unlike multi-cultural education, these approaches do not seek to relate information about minority groups. These approaches generally seek to encourage empathy, perspective-taking and thinking about prejudice. As a result, narrative story telling rather than the use of factual information is the dominant tool. Typically, the mode of administration is reading material, theatre, film or teacher/peer-led discussion. Although the impact of such approaches is not as well documented as those of some others, they have scored some notable successes and the documented outcomes are generally positive. Positive outcomes have been reported with the use of stories (Cameron and Rutland, 2006), soap operas (Paluck, 2009) and peer influence (Paluck, 2006).

Cooperative learning, multi-cultural curricula and social–cognitive skills training represent three different rich and complex traditions for dealing with problematic inter-ethnic relations among children. Each exhibits some kind of intuitive appeal (we can reduce prejudice by proper contact with other ethnic groups, by learning about them, by seeing the world from their perspective and by thinking about our own prejudices). Each approach has a broader educational significance in that each addresses the acquisition of important knowledge about the world and/or transferable skills. As a suite of approaches, they also offer the advantage that some require the presence of minority members while others do not. We believe that each approach has something to offer, but that a great deal of caution is necessary. The results for all approaches are mixed. How they will perform in the context of the rapid increase in diversity which Ireland has experienced is unclear. Much of the available evidence comes from American studies of interaction between black and white pupils. It is unclear how these approaches will deal with the kinds of layered difference in cultural and social outlook discussed in Chapter 5, how they will work in the context of the often harsh realities of social disadvantage, and how they can be implemented on a large scale. Finally, it is worth noting that all of these approaches presume a common language in which children can communicate with one another. We believe that these three traditions are by far the best alternatives currently available for addressing general issues to do with inter-cultural contact, but we would also stress that a lot of serious attention needs to be given to realities of what can be implemented in an Irish context and how.

As a final note in this section, we wish to consider two other issues that arose in this research: racial bullying and the transmission of racist attitudes to children by adults. Neither of these issues is directly addressed by the three traditions discussed above, although they all do have a bearing. Increased social cohesion should have an impact on bullying, while greater knowledge and cognitive processing should impact on pre-existing prejudices. However, we can also think about these two issues in a more specific way. Racial bullying can be considered within the more general framework of anti-bullying initiatives. Numerous anti-bullying programmes have been developed which have been shown to be effective in reducing bullying. Some examples include the Norwegian Zero programme (Roland and

Munthe, 1997), the Olweus Bullying Prevention Program (Olweus, 1997, 2005), and the Irish ABC programme (O'Moore and Minton, 2004). We have been unable to find any initiatives which specifically target the inter-generational transmission of racist attitudes, but it would seem to provide a focused target for intervention, the aim not being to reduce adult racism *per se* but to discourage the rehearsal of racist attitudes in the presence of children.

Existing Policy and Practice in Ireland

Although Irish integration policy is the responsibility of various departments of state, the most important for our present purpose is the Department of Education and Skills. While the Education Act (1998) committed to respecting diversity in Irish society, in practice the two most important policy documents which specifically responded to the increased multi-culturalism of Irish primary schools are:

- Circular 0053/2007 by the Department of Education and Science
- 'Intercultural Education in the Primary School' by the National Council for Curriculum Assessment (2005).

The date of these two policy documents is worth noting as they both emerged after the demographic changes that migration brought to Ireland (late 1990s onwards). This is not a criticism. The scale of migration and especially migration of children was not clear for some time and detailed policy responses take time to develop. The dates are significant because they highlight the fact that schools had little central leadership to respond to the challenges of migration in its early years. There was, therefore, a period in which schools developed their own strategies for dealing with the challenges that migration brought, before any properly formulated guidance or support was available. Such 'home-grown' practices can become embedded as relatively powerful routines quite quickly.

Where To from Here? Policy Challenges   175

As discussed in Chapter 5, English language competence is essential for social integration of migrant children into Irish schools and society. As we have also made clear, however, it is does not guarantee social acceptance or integration, but it is an absolutely vital prerequisite for either.

Circular 0053/2007 outlined a series of provisions to provide English language instruction on a withdrawal basis, i.e. newcomer children who require it are withdrawn from normal classes to learn English in a separate class. Schools were offered financial assistance (to support teaching staff) depending on the number of newcomer students enrolled.

The provisions of Circular 0053/2007 for English language support have been criticised for its 'one size fits all' approach (Lyons and Little, 2009), but the initiative did represent a significant investment on the part of the State, costing in the region of €120 million per annum. Since 2009, the programme has been cut back with the loss of approximately 500 English language support teachers across both the primary and secondary systems. Teachers unions have been critical and predict a drop in the quality and quantity of service provided to migrant pupils.

The intercultural education guidelines relate even more directly to the issues of social integration which we have discussed in this book. The guidelines were published in 2005 and include a broad range of materials and suggestions designed to promote an inter-cultural atmosphere in schools. The overarching principle is that of inter-culturalism. In terms of the strategies for reducing inter-ethnic prejudice outlined in the previous section, it most closely relates to those labelled 'social–cognitive skills' training. The guidelines contain some very valuable and detailed information including:

- Background sections for teachers which explain the demography of migration into Ireland and discuss the benefits of inter-cultural education.

- A discussion of school level planning for inter-cultural education, including the role of parents and communities.

- Detailed recommendations for class planning and how to positively recognise various forms of diversity in the classroom. The use of cooperative learning is endorsed. Detailed, age appropriate, lesson plans are provided including materials designed to counter ethnocentrism and encourage perspective taking and empathy. Strategies for identifying inter-cultural opportunities across the whole curriculum are discussed.

- Strategies to encourage active learning.

- A review of issues to do with assessment in multi-cultural classrooms.

The guidelines provide the most detailed and comprehensive set of materials available for those schools that are adapting to the changed social realities brought about by migration. We will return to the use to which the guidelines may be put later. Let us first consider a few issues which they raise that require clarification and development:

- The guidelines appear to be completely untested in an Irish context. The guidelines present themselves with a beguiling authority, but international experience would warn us to be cautious in assuming that, if implemented, these educational practices would produce profound attitudinal change, let alone the kinds of positive behavioural changes within the child's social space that were listed in our aims above.

- The guidelines do not seriously address themselves to unique features of the Irish migration experience, such as the wide range of nationalities and diversity involved, or the unusual educational profile of migrants to Ireland. As we have seen, these issues can have a profound impact on social interaction among children.

- The issue of how individual schools are to deal with unusually challenging circumstances, such as in some cases serious ethnic tension in the local catchment area, is not addressed.

Where To from Here? Policy Challenges 177

- How the guidelines were developed is not clear. They do not appear to be a response to particular issues that have arisen, but are based on a digest of international literature and the kinds of problems that generally occur. General problems such as stereotyping and ethnocentrism are a reality with which they deal, but serious racial bullying is not.

- The use of cooperative learning is endorsed, but the examples given are quite general and, if examined closely, bear little resemblance to cooperative learning as it is described in the educational literature. What the examples given most resemble is group work as it is normally practiced in schools in Ireland. Cooperative learning properly defined is a highly specialised and specific form of teaching which for theoretical reasons is believed to substantially improve inter-group relations. It requires training for teachers before it can be administered properly.

- No funding or support was provided to sponsor the implementation of the guidelines. The actual extent to which they have been implemented is currently unclear. In our own fieldwork, we have never encountered them or heard them mentioned by a teacher or school principal.

Having said this, 'Intercultural Education in the Primary School' is a very important document. It embodies key values, provides plenty of useful advice and offers ready-made intercultural lesson plans. If we are to think seriously about how schools might adequately adjust to the new realities of multi-cultural Ireland and the kinds of problems identified earlier, the guidelines are a very useful starting point.

Schools themselves have, of course, been responding to the increase in migration since it began. In their national survey of schools, Smyth, Darmody, McGinnity and Byrne (2009) found that the likelihood of a school having a formal written policy on inter-culturalism or anti-racism varied as a function of the proportion of newcomer students in the school. Approximately 60 per cent of schools with a migrant population greater than 20 per cent had such a policy. For schools with no migrant pupils, the same figure was approximately 20 per cent. The basis or effectiveness of such policies is not known. The Smyth, Darmody, McGinnity and Byrne (2009) survey also looks at measures to support newcomer students in primary schools. The most common of these is provision of books, followed by financial assistance for trips and 'extracurricular activities'.

Anti-bullying policy is also of particular relevance to the issue of racial bullying. Since 1990, the Department of Education and Science pursued a policy of encouraging all primary and secondary schools to develop their own anti-bullying policy (Department of Education, 1993). No funding or support was provided and school level adaptation of anti-bullying policy appears to have been patchy until schools were legally obliged to adopt a formal anti-bullying policy under the Education (Welfare) Act, 2000. A study of the ABC (Anti-Bullying Centre) anti-bullying programme in 42 schools in Ireland found it to be very effective in reducing bullying. However, when the programme was rolled out on a national basis its effectiveness was greatly reduced (Minton and O'Moore, 2008). The authors attribute the loss of effectiveness to implementation issues. The national survey of schools by Smyth, Darmody, McGinnity and Byrne (2009) found that all schools taking part in their study had an anti-bullying policy in place, but that racial bullying was only covered under the policies of 40 per cent of primary schools. In practice, we might expect that the two major issues that need to be addressed in relation to anti-bullying policy are how and when such policy is implemented and how it relates specifically to racial bullying. In the present research, quite serious examples of racial bullying were seen to slip under the radar. We encountered no success stories in terms of managing bullying issues which had been resolved by anyone other than the children themselves. Racial bullying presents quite serious challenges in terms of the harm that it causes, whether and how it gets reported, and the training required to deal with it effectively and confidently.

Possibilities of Implementing New Policies and Practices in Ireland

Our ultimate aim is to develop a range of measures to improve the inter-cultural environment of multi-cultural schools in Ireland. These measures would be selected and developed on the basis of their demonstrated effectiveness and feasibility. We recognise that given the huge range of demands on teachers in Ireland, the implementation of any new measures should be as undemanding as possible. We will explore these issues further through a series of questions:

What would this 'range of measures' look like?

On the basis of our preceding discussion, we might predict that an ideal package would include:

- Some use of cooperative learning

- A limited amount of multi-cultural curriculum

- Social–cognitive skills training

- An extension of anti-bullying policy to cover racial bullying and a tightening up of the enforcement of that policy.

What do we mean by 'shown to be effective in improving the inter-cultural environment of multi-cultural schools in Ireland'?

Evaluating policies is crucial. It is only in confronting the realities of particular schools, communities, children and teachers that we can know which strategies are effective under which conditions and how these strategies may be improved. The alternative to evaluation can be seductive, but it is ultimately shallow and potentially misleading. It is the issuing of general, untested recommendations to all schools everywhere. It can create the impression of urgency (the deed is done in the doing) and effectiveness (who is to say it is not effective?) but the presumption of effectiveness is only apparent. A close reading of the international literature does not encourage optimism. Recommendations can cause harm as well as good by their implementation, while the realities addressed are complex and varied. Without a close eye on implementation, general recommendations may be opening the door to tokenism and simply be distracting from more serious efforts to improve the situation. It may be the case that evaluation of 'on the ground' initiatives in even one school may produce more profound insight and progress than any form of desk-based speculation and prescription.

There is of course pressure on all sides for the different parties involved (including researchers) to appear to be doing their job well. A general and mutual recognition that we are faced with very profound challenges seems to be the best way of creating meaningful dialogue. This is not a justification for doing nothing, but a basis for open and intelligent discussion. As things stand, we do not have the authority to say what will be effective in the Irish context, but we do not believe anyone else has either. The evidence is simply not there. When it is, we expect it will reveal a much more complex and interesting picture than anything we might expect. The counter-argument is, can we wait to evaluate? The answer is, not really. That is why we should start as soon as possible. There is a very long and difficult road ahead and the sooner we start the better.

How should evaluation take place?

A variety of schools should be selected and supported to implement designated policies. These schools effectively become 'model' multi-cultural schools. The experience of schools, teachers and children in implementing these policies should be evaluated qualitatively. One-to-one or two-child interviews are particularly to be recommended over focus groups as children may be able to talk more frankly about embarrassing experiences they may have had without peers present. The impact of these policies should also be evaluated through the use of validated survey data. A crucial element in high quality evaluations is comparing such data with that from sites which have had no new policies introduced. The use of comparison points like this is crucial as we know that

Where To from Here? Policy Challenges   181

phenomena such as inter-ethnic interaction can change over time regardless of any changes in practice. Comparisons are the only way we have of being sure that improvements observed can be attributed to the new policies and not to the passage of time. In relation to measurement, a crucial lesson from the present research is the importance of age-appropriate approaches to research which tap into the realities of the child's social world.

What is meant by ensuring 'that schools and teachers have to do as little as possible to implement'?

Teachers are crucial in implementing the policies we are discussing and, in our experience, teachers already have plenty to be doing. We can presume that, all other things being equal, those policies are most likely to be implemented which require least effort or least sense of 'pushing against the stream'. Therefore, we should do as much as possible to ensure that proposed changes are as streamlined and easy to implement as possible. How this would work in practice cannot be elaborated in too much detail here. However, we might expect detailed development and testing of lesson plans before they are offered to teachers and schools. Initial training is required in the case of techniques like cooperative learning. This should be provided pre-implementation and to existing school principals and teachers.

What happens then?

When policies have been tried and tested in 'model' schools and found to be effective, the materials may be refined in the light of experience and disseminated across the school system nationally. The mode of distribution would most likely be training sessions at schools and a website where teachers can download materials (on the model of the excellent **www.elsp.ie** website, which provides teachers with English language support teaching materials). Obviously, this will not be enough to ensure nationwide implementation in multi-cultural schools, but it will be a valuable start. The presence of actual viable models can be very powerful. There is something concrete and evidence-based to rally behind.

The next stage is lobbying policy makers and individual schools to implement the policy. Discussing the challenges which face the implementation of the ABC anti-bullying programme in Ireland, Midtassel, Minton, and O'Moore (2009) emphasise the importance of the role of national authorities in promoting a programme through 'their focus, legislation and resource allocation'. They also draw attention to the importance of school level planning and programme delivery.

Who is going to pay?
This is clearly a key question, but we would make two points. What we are proposing is (a) comparatively speaking not that expensive and (b) the responsibility and remit of many different governmental and non-governmental agencies.

There are two final issues to be considered in relation to implementation. Firstly, it is worth reminding ourselves of the experience of School 6 in our research. This highlights the fact that some schools may face much more serious challenges than others, especially those which are located in communities in which ethnic tension is very high. These schools, once identified, may require special attention and support. In this section on implementation, we have focused solely on the education system. This is largely because this has been the focus in most international research in this area. However, clearly the broader community has an important role to play. At a very minimum, the issue of the transmission of prejudice from adults to children needs to be looked at.

We believe that openness, moderation and a willingness to engage with the messy realities of inter-cultural contact is also crucial for those of us who would shape, propose or implement policies in relation to integration. There are stances to be avoided: the belief that migration will go away; that this all has nothing to with education; that the optimum policy was formulated by schools responding reactively to the challenges of migration; that we will reach Berlin by Christmas. Also to be avoided is the belief that we can select policies and practices from other contexts and

Where To from Here? Policy Challenges 183

effect positive change by scattering their wisdom to the winds without examining the consequences of those policies and practices in the current Irish context. A reluctance to record the outcomes of policies even in quite limited and select locations is based on an unrealistic and unwholesome logic, an ironic re-enactment of prejudiced mentality.

Chapter 9

Where To from Here? Possible Futures for Inter-ethnic Relations in Ireland

In this chapter, we review the main findings and arguments of the book and discuss their implications for the future of inter-ethnic relations in Ireland.

The global recession has seen many migrants leaving Ireland. As yet exact figures are not available. The year up to April 2010 witnessed the highest level of net migration out of Ireland since 1989 (CSO, 2010). However, this change is in a large part due to a substantial increase in the number of Irish nationals emigrating. Nationals of the EU12 accession states emigrated from Ireland in large numbers in 2009, but since then the number leaving has decreased considerably. Numbers from the rest of the world (excluding UK and EU15) emigrating from Ireland increased slightly in 2009 and have remained constant since then. The exact numbers of migrants currently resident in Ireland will not be known until after Census 2011. However international experience tells us that, for a variety of reasons, migrants often do not simply leave when circumstances change. This will be especially true in the case of a global recession and for migrants with school-going children. Not all jobs are lost, roots and connections are made, and opportunities may be limited or non-existent elsewhere. We predict that multi-culturalism will be a feature of many schools in Ireland for a very long time to come. As such, it is an issue that it is important we address fully and constructively as soon as possible.

Possible Futures for Inter-ethnic Relations in Ireland 185

This research presented us with an in-depth look at inter-ethnic relations among children in a large part of central Dublin. A number of key issues emerging were:

- Schools and communities in the inner-city experienced a sudden increase in the number and diversity of children from a migrant background over a relatively short period of time from the late 1990s onwards.

- Some forms of social interaction which occur within the child's social sphere can be difficult for parents and teachers to observe.

- As well as cultural differences, migrant and local children often differ from one another in terms of their social values and home life. In general, migrant children in Dublin's north inner-city appear to be more studious, ambitious, conservative and better supported in their education by their parents than their local peers.

- While there is some positive interaction between migrant and local children, this is generally limited in terms of who is involved and in what they are involved.

- A common feature of social interaction between migrant and local children is an 'intentional separateness', a desire among the children to stay with what is familiar and to avoid social contact with the other cultural group.

- Local children exhibited some hostility in relation to other countries and to adult migrants. These included general stereotypical beliefs about foreign countries and in some cases prejudiced beliefs about migrants. These beliefs could sometimes be extremely intense and in some cases seemed to be influenced by the views of adults.

- The inter-cultural climate evident in each school varied quite dramatically between the schools.

- Aside from the everyday 'roughness' and more targeted bullying which is often part of life in Irish schools, a clear strand of racially motivated bullying is identifiable. Racism can occur both in and out of school. This usually takes the form of (isolated or more persistent) ethnic name-calling, but can also involve physical assault.

• In some more serious cases of racial bullying that our fieldworkers observed, there is unambiguous evidence of psychological harm.

This is, of course, a case study of seven schools in one area. The logic of case study research is not that findings from one site translate simply from that site to another, but that findings from different sites can mutually inform one another. We expect that experiences will vary by context. But given the broad range of issues covered, we would also predict that similar research, in other parts of Ireland with high concentrations of migrant children, would encounter similar issues to a greater or lesser extent. As discussed in the preceding chapters, with the exception of the more serious forms of bullying, many of the broad findings from this study have been corroborated by other Irish studies. The fact that more ethnic bullying was reported in the current study may be due to methodological and regional differences. Regardless of how these findings will 'travel', the north inner-city is a large and important site in its own right. It has attracted many migrants and will most likely continue to do so. There is every reason to believe that multi-culturalism is now a permanent feature of the social landscape of the inner-city given the very high concentrations of migrants currently living there.

Where might we expect these children to go from here? Attempting to answer this is, of course, speculative and will depend on many different factors. However, we can make a number of observations. The primary school, and in particular the Irish primary school, is in many respects an ideal site for children from different cultural backgrounds to engage with one another. It is the one site in which children regularly interact in both structured and unstructured environments. Primary schools generally have a stable class composition and a warm,

Possible Futures for Inter-ethnic Relations in Ireland   187

constructive atmosphere. When these children enter secondary school, they will encounter a more hectic, fluid and competitive environment. If children have not had positive experiences of cross-cultural friendships in primary school, it is arguable that they are even less likely to find these in the potentially more daunting atmosphere of secondary school. In such a hypothetical future, we might expect that separateness becomes an even more prominent note, leading to communities of young people living parallel to rather than integrated with one another.

Integration, in the formal sense, need not mean constant engagement or loss of identity, but rather reflects knowledge and acceptance of different cultures (Berry, 2001). The will to keep apart, to not bother, to stay with what is comfortable tends to lead to a lack of engagement. The net effect is cultural 'silos', parallel communities within communities. Some consequences we might expect from such distance between cultural communities are a certain distrust, misapprehension and lack of realistic knowledge. Aside from the purely negative effects, we must also consider the positive experiences which will be lost. In psychological research, 'integration' – a positive identification with one's own culture and an openness to others – has been identified as the healthiest approach to inter-cultural interaction. For migrant children, close knowledge of wider society is an invaluable asset. For local children, experience of other cultures represents an opportunity for learning about the world, broadening horizons and acquiring transferable social skills. Failure to interact across cultural difference may lead to lost potential for both sides.

If we hypothesise that separateness will be a dominant feature of inter-cultural relations among this group of children, we can also predict that the experiences of some children will be quite different. On the one hand, we can expect pockets of cordial, warm and even very close cross-ethnic contact to occur. The maintenance and development of such positive relationships is in some respects supported by factors within the broader social context. For example, to date, cultural assimilation (the view that migrants should adopt Irish culture) is generally not part of the local expectations in relation to migration. Strong Dublin accents that are encountered among some of this generation of migrant youth tend to be met with bemusement rather than any expectation that this is the way it should be. Furthermore, there is no significant anti-immigration platform in Irish politics. Integration (in the original sense of mutual cultural recognition proposed by Berry, 2001) is stated government and City Council policy, a position that is supported by all the major political parties. Arguably, other forces supporting a respect for cultural distinctiveness in Ireland may include a history of colonisation and emigration, the overwhelming diversity of the migrant population and the mobile nature of modern migration. Aside from these issues, the inner-city is a rich and historic community with a lot of diversity in its own right. Alongside a certain reserve and a history of hardship and deprivation, there can be sudden sympathy, warmth and humour which can be the basis of lasting friendship and respectful interaction.

On the other hand, we encountered many negatives in this research: ethnocentrism, prejudiced beliefs, racism and bullying. Such attitudes and experiences inevitably have an impact and a legacy that may be felt long into the future. As we discussed, ethnocentrism is almost universal among human beings and the strain that we encountered in our research (which presents the 'western world' as civilised and advanced and the rest of the world as backward, war-torn and famished) is a very common one among all classes of society. This should not lead us to underestimate its importance. Such beliefs provide an unrealistic basis for inter-cultural relations which can blind people even to realities which confront them directly. At best they lead to a condescending attitude, at worst avoidance and alienation. Prejudice is a natural outgrowth and we can expect that many children will continue, or come to hold, prejudiced attitudes. Evidence in the present research of direct and indirect exposure to the prejudiced beliefs of adults is a worrying finding. Inter-generational transmission can be a very powerful force main-taining prejudice in a community (Duriez and Soenens, 2009). We

Possible Futures for Inter-ethnic Relations in Ireland   189

also found that such attitudes can be site-specific with particular areas or communities appearing to experience much more severe difficulties than others. We can expect that racial bullying, name-calling and stigmatisation will continue to be features of the social landscape for the children who took part in our research as they grow up. The likely reactions to such behavior are predictable – physical and mental health problems, resentment and anger. We must also consider the long-term consequences of the serious bullying to which a minority of migrant children are currently being exposed. So if we predict that distance and separation will be a dominant feature, we must also assume that some darker currents will also be present. Even if regular engagement and exposure to very negative attitudes and behaviours is confined to a minority of young people, the consequences of such exposure may still be very serious. Firstly, there is physical and psychological harm that is caused which can be far more profound than people may wish to acknowledge. Secondly, even a relatively small number of migrant and local children engaged in very negative forms of interaction may have a profound impact on the broader social context. Extreme negative events such as racial assaults or bullying-related suicides can attract enormous public attention and have an effect on attitudes reaching far beyond the people who were immediately involved in an incident.

In summary, the future of inter-ethnic relations among the children who took part in our research may be one in which integration is a drab failure, where distance and separation predominate and cultural communities live parallel to, rather than with, one another. In places, the resilience, warmth and energy of both local and migrant communities may flourish into friendly interaction and, on occasion, close friendship. In other places, prejudice and racism could lead to deep and harmful divisions. The long-term implications of such a pattern are hard to envisage, but optimism of any description seems unwarranted. As discussed in the last chapter, the way forward we propose is one in which:

- The realities of children's own social spaces are taken seriously.

- Evidence-based intervention strategies to enhance inter-ethnic relations are developed in Irish contexts.

- There is rigorous qualitative and quantitative evaluation of such strategies in multi-cultural Irish schools with a view to developing models of best practice and a detailed body of evidence-based policy.

When we think about the future of the children who took part in our study, another issue is what the future holds for these children in terms of employment and social mobility? Among the migrant children, a spirit of ambition and wanting to do well clearly shines through. As migrant children grow up, their views will change depending on their experiences in society, their educational attainments and their occupational success. The generation which follows them may have quite different views and experiences. International research on second generation migrants is voluminous and mixed. Some thrive and integrate more deeply than their predecessors, others do less well and/or withdraw from the mainstream society in which they live. To some degree, this will again depend on their experiences in society and their occupational and educational success. Some groups have experienced upward mobility (for example, the Irish in the US) while in other cases, enthusiasm and ambition have been lost in the face of lack of opportunity and discrimination producing a so-called second generation decline. Experience has varied greatly by country (Hernandez, Macartney and Blanchard, 2009), ethnic group (Portes and Rumbaut, 2001) and even by the type of upward mobility that we look at. How this will play out in the Irish context is not yet at all clear, but one thing is certain: for better or worse, the second generation will be different from the first.

In both this study and in other Irish research, it has been noted that the presence of academically ambitious migrant children has changed the tenor of many schools and classrooms. Teachers have noted that the performance of migrant children puts pressure on local children to do well. All in all, a quite remarkable change has

Possible Futures for Inter-ethnic Relations in Ireland   191

happened: schools have had an influx of ambitious and able students. This is a development that would be impossible to engineer and something which should be viewed as a great opportunity for schools in historically disadvantaged areas like the north inner-city. This generation represents an opportune moment for investment as the situation may not continue for long.

In this book we have attempted to look 'under the skin' of inter-ethnic relations in the lives of children attending primary school in Dublin's north inner-city. At times, we have perhaps focused on the negatives. These, we believe, are very real and deserving of urgent attention. Working with the children themselves was an enriching experience and we hope this comes through in the small selection of quotations we have presented. We believe that there are grounds for hope and optimism and that, on the whole, migration has brought great opportunities to areas such as Dublin's north inner-city. The extent to which those opportunities are realised is the question. We have seen children with open tolerant attitudes and ambitious, able, hard-working children. We have also seen serious fault lines in the social fabric of these communities of children.

Throughout this book we have focused on the lives of children. We have touched on the way in which some of their attitudes and experiences may have been shaped by adults but have not pursued this topic far, as it was not the focus of our research. But the issues discussed in this book have a wider social significance. There is pervasive evidence that these are issues that Irish society as a whole struggles to come to terms with. Survey data on the views of Irish adults suggest that many hold negative stereotypical images of migrants (O'Connell and Winston, 2006). A field-experiment by McGinnity, Nelson, Lunn and Quinn (2009) found that Irish employers exhibited strong discrimination against job applicants simply on the basis of having a non-Irish name. Children may not be the only ones who perceive themselves as separate from migrants or feel hostility towards them. They may, however, be the ones who speak about it more frankly.

Appendix

The Children, Youth and Community Relations Research Programme

Background

The Children, Youth and Community Relations Research Programme of Trinity Immigration Initiative is based at the Children's Research Centre, Trinity College Dublin. It aims to promote more positive experiences of immigration and intercultural encounters for both immigrant and 'local' children and young people, as they adapt to culturally diverse schools and neighbourhoods. The Children, Youth and Community Relations Research Programme proceeds on the assumption that many of the seeds of success in this effort for successful integration can be laid in the formative attitudes and experiences of children and young people who are part of the migration experience, whether as migrants or as those who encounter migrants. The Programme wishes to contribute sound evidence in this area to inform public debate, policy and practice at local and national levels. To this end, it investigates:

- The experiences of young immigrants

- The experiences of young people on both sides of the cultural encounter in contexts of cultural diversity

- The evidence on international best practice for schools in promoting positive intercultural relations between young people from different cultural backgrounds

194   *Where To from Here?*

- Resources necessary for supporting schools in managing the opportunities and challenges presented by a more diverse student base

- The support needs and service experiences of young immigrants and their families.

Research Activities

As well as the research discussed in this book, the programme has also completed a study of the experiences of life in Ireland of 169 young immigrants aged 15-17 from across the country. This research was co-sponsored and co-funded by Integrating Ireland, the NGO that has now amalgamated with Refugee Information Service to form the Integration Centre. The report on this research can be downloaded from: **http://www.tcd.ie/immigration/css/ downloads/In_the_front_line_of_Integration.pdf**

Work is almost complete on a systematic review of the use of cooperative learning to promote positive inter-ethnic relations. This work has been done in association with the international Campbell Collaboration which is an international network of researchers committed to producing robust syntheses of research evidence to support policy development and decisions. A rigorous process of peer review governs every study admitted to the Campbell programme. The study is supported by a grant from the Irish Research Council on Humanities and Social Sciences.

We have recently been awarded funding by the Irish Research Council for the Humanities and Social Sciences to support a knowledge exchange project of the results of the research presented in this book with key stakeholder groups such as schools, teachers and policy makers.

Post-graduate Students

We currently have three PhD students working on our project:

1. Lindsey Garratt is exploring the impact of the body in the development of positive and negative relationships between migrant and majority group boys. The effect of physical

competence in sport and racialised body phenotypes are being examined to explore integration as a lived social relation. Lindsey's work is funded by the Office of the Minister for Children and Youth Affairs.

2. Jennifer Scholtz is researching the impact of immigration on immigrant young girls' everyday experiences and how this influences their interactions and relationships with others. She is investigating how children negotiate identity, difference and belonging within their social networks. Jenny's work is funded by the Family Support Agency.

3. Kate Babineau is conducting a quantitative, cross-sectional survey of children's perspectives on peer relations in multi-ethnic Irish primary schools.

Keep up-to-date with all of our work at: **http://www.tcd.ie/ immigration/community.**

References

Aboud, F. (1988) *Children and Prejudice*. Oxford: Blackwell.

Aboud, F. (2005). 'The development of prejudice in childhood and adolescence.' In J.F. Dovidio, P. Glick and L. Rudman (eds.), *On the Nature of Prejudice: Fifty Years after Allport*. Malden, MA: Blackwell Publishing.

Aboud, F. and Levy, S. (2000), 'Interventions to reduce prejudice in children and adolescents', in *Reducing Prejudice and Discrimination*, Mahwah, New Jersey: Lawrence Erlbaum Associates Inc., pp. 269–94.

Allport, G.W. (1954). *The Nature of Prejudice*. Cambridge, MA: Addison-Wesley.

Amin, S. (1988). *Eurocentrism*. London: Zed.

Aronson, E. (1978). *The Jigsaw Classroom*. Beverley Hills, CA: Sage.

Aronson, E. and Osherow, N. (1980). 'Cooperation, pro-social behaviour and academic performance. Experiments in the desegregated classroom'. In L. Bickman (ed.), *Applied Social Psychology* (Vol. 1, pp. 163-197). Newbury Park, CA: Sage.

Aronson, E. and Patnoe, S. (1997). *The Jigsaw Classroom*, New York: Longman.

Bannon, M.J., Eustace, J.G. and O'Neill, M. (1981) *Urbanisation: Problems of Growth and Decay in Dublin*, National Economic and Social Council Report No. 55, Dublin: Stationery Office.

Barrett, A., Bergin, A. and Duffy, D. (2006). 'The labour market characteristics of labour market impacts of immigrants in Ireland'. *Economic and Social Review*, 37 (1), 1-26.

Barrett, A. and Kelly, E. (2008) 'How Reliable is the Quarterly National Household Survey for Migration Research?', *Economic and Social Review*, Vol. 39, No. 3, Winter 2008, pp. 191–205.

Berry, J.W. (2001). 'A psychology of immigration'. *Journal of Social Issues*, 57, 615-631.

Bigler, R.S. (1999). 'The use of multicultural curricula and materials to counter racism in children'. *Journal of Social Issues*, 55, 687–705.

Binder, J., Zagefka, H., Brown, R., Funke, F., Kessler, T., Mummendey, A. et al. (2009). 'Does contact reduce prejudice or does prejudice reduce contact? A longitudinal test of the contact hypothesis among majority and minority groups in three European countries'. *Journal of Personality and Social Psychology* 96 (4), 843-856.

Blaney, N.T., Stephen, C., Rosenfield, D., Aronson, E. and Sikes, J. (1977). 'Interdependence in the classroom: A field study'. *Journal of Educational Psychology*, 69 (2), 121-128.

Bowling, A. (2002) *Research Methods in Health* (2nd Ed.). Open University Press.

Brown, R., and Hewstone, M. (2005). 'An integrative theory of intergroup contact'. In *Advances in Experimental Social Psychology* (Vol. 37, pp. 255-343). San Diego, CA, US: Elsevier Academic Press.

Cameron, L. and Rutland, A. (2006) 'Extended contact through story reading in school: Reducing children's prejudice towards the disabled'. *Journal of Social Issues*, 62, 469–88.

Cameron, J.A., Alvarez, J.M., Ruble, D.N. and Fuligni, A.J. (2001). 'Children's lay theories about ingroups and outgroups: Reconceptualizing research on prejudice', *Personality and Social Psychology Review*, 5 (2), 118-128.

Carney, M., Chamberlain, J., Garvey, C., McGee, P. and Quinn, P. (1970) Rutland Street Research Project (unpublished) Dublin: Department of Psychology, University College Dublin.

Central Statistics Office (2003). *Census 2002: Principal Demographic Results.* Stationery Office: Dublin.

Central Statistics Office (2008). *Census 2006: Non-nationals living in Ireland.* Stationery Office: Dublin.

References

Central Statistics Office (2009). *Population and Migration Estimates.* Stationery Office: Dublin.

Central Statistics Office (2010). *Population and Migration Estimates.* The Stationery Office: Dublin.

Coakley, L. and Mac Einri, P. (2007). *The Integration Experiences of African Families in Ireland.* Dublin: Integrating Ireland.

Clark, K.B. and Clark, M.K. (1939). 'The development of consciousness of self and the emergence of racial identification in negro preschool children'. *Journal of Social Psychology,* 10, 591-599.

Clark, K.B. and Clark, M.P. (1947). Racial identification and preference in Negro children. In T.M. Newcomb and E.L. Hartley (eds.), *Readings in social psychology.* New York: Holt, pp. 168-78.

Cocks, A.J (2006) 'The Ethical Maze: Finding an inclusive path towards gaining children's agreement to research participation', *Childhood,* 13 (2), 247-266.

Cohen, E. (1986). *Designing Groupwork: Strategies for the Heterogeneous Classroom.* New York: Teachers College Press.

Cohen, E.G., Bianchini, J.A., Cossey, R., Holthuis, N.C., Morphew, C.C. and Whitcomb, J.A. (1997). 'What did students learn?' In E.G. Cohen and R.A. Lotan (eds.), *Working for Equity in Heterogeneous Classrooms: Sociological Theory in Practice* (pp. 137-165). New York: Teacher College Press.

Cohen, E.G., Lockheed, M., and Lohman, M. (1976). 'The Center for Interracial Cooperation: A field experiment'. *Sociology of Education,* 49, 47-58.

Cohen, E.G. and Lotan, R.A. (1995). 'Producing equal status interaction in the heterogeneous classroom'. *American Educational Research Journal* 32, 99-120.

Cohen, E.G. and Lotan, R.A. (eds.). (1997). *Working for Equity in Heterogenenous Classrooms: Sociological Theory in Practice.* New York: Teachers College Press.

Cohen, E.G. and Roper, S. (1972). 'Modification of interracial interaction disability: An application of status characteristics theory'. *American Sociological Review* 37, 648-655.

Connolly, P., Smith, A. and Kelly, B. (2002) *Too Young to Notice? The Cultural and Political Awareness of 3-6 Year Olds in Northern Ireland.* Belfast: Northern Ireland Community Relations Council.

Cook, T. and Hess. E. (2007) 'What the Camera Sees and from Whose Perspective: Fun methodologies for engaging children in enlightening adults' *Childhood,* 14 (1), 29-45.

Cooper, R. and Slavin, R.E. (2004). 'Cooperative learning: An instructional strategy to improve intergroup relations'. In W.G. Stephan and W.P. Vogt (eds.), *Education Programs for Improving Intergroup Relations* (p. 323). New York: Teachers College Press.

Creswell, J.W. (1998). *Qualitative Inquiry and Research Design: Choosing among Five Traditions.* Thousand Oaks, CA: Sage.

Davis, P. (2007) 'Storytelling as a democratic approach to data collection: Interviewing children about reading' in *Educational Research* 49, 2.

Denzin, N.K. (1978). *The Research Act: A Theoretical Introduction to Sociological Methods.* New York: McGraw-Hill.

Denzin, N. (2006). *Sociological Methods: A Sourcebook (5th Ed.).* Aldine Transaction.

Department of Education (1993). Guidelines on Countering Bullying Behaviour in Primary and Post-Primary Schools. Dublin: DOE.

Department of Education (2010). Social Inclusion – Programmes and Schemes – Delivering Equality of Opportunity in Schools (DEIS). http://www.education.ie/robots/view.jsp?pcategory=17216andlanguage= ENandecategory=33128 [Accessed on 19/11/2010]

Deutsch, M. (1949). 'A theory of cooperation and competition'. *Human Relations,* 2, 129-151.

Deutsch, M. (1962) 'Cooperation and trust: Some theoretical notes'. In M.R. Jones (ed.), *Nebraska Symposium on Motivation* (pp. 275-319). Lincoln: University of Nebraska Press.

Devine, D. (2005) 'Welcome to the Celtic Tiger? Teacher responses to immigration and increasing ethnic diversity in Irish schools'. *International Studies in Sociology of Education,* 15 (1), 49-70.

Devine, D. (2009) 'Mobilising capitals? Migrant children's negotiation of their everyday lives in the primary school'. *British Journal of Sociology of Education,* 30 (5).

References

Devine, D. (2011) *Immigration and Dchooling in Ireland – Making a Difference?* Manchester: Manchester University Press.

Devine, D. and Kenny, M. (2002) *Ethnicity and Schooling A study of ethnic diversity in selected Irish primary and post-primary schools;* Commissioned report for the Department of Education and Science.

Devine, D. with Kelly, M. (2006) '"I just don't want to get picked on by anybody" – Dynamics of inclusion and exclusion in a newly multi-ethnic Irish primary school'. *Children and Society*, 20 (2), 128-139.

Devine, D., Kenny, M. and MacNeela, E. (2008) '"Naming the Other' – children's construction and experience of racisms in Irish primary schools'. *Race Ethnicity and Education*, 11 (4), 369-385.

DeVries, D. and Edwards, K. (1974). 'Student teams and learning games: Their effects on cross-race and cross-sex interaction'. *Journal of Educational Psychology*, 66, 741-749.

De Vries, D.L., Slavin, R.E., Fennessey, G.M., Edwards, K.J. and Lombardo, M.M. (1980). *Teams-games Tournament. The Team Learning Approach.* Englewood Cliffs, NJ: Educational Technology Publications.

Duriez, B. and Soenens, B. (2009). 'The intergenerational transmission of racism: The role of right-wing authoritarianism and social dominance orientation'. *Journal of Research in Personality*, 43, 906-909.

Eivers, E., Shiel G. and Cunnignham, R. (2007). *Ready for Tomorrow's World? The Competencies of Irish 15-year-olds in PISA 2006. Main report.* Dublin: Educational Research Centre.

Fanning, B., Haase, T. and O'Boyle, N. (2011) 'Well-being, Cultural Capital and Social Inclusion: Immigrants in the Republic of Ireland'. *Journal of International Migration and Integration,* 12, 1-24.

Germain, R. (2004) 'An exploratory study using cameras and Talking Mats to access the views of young people with learning disabilities on their out-of-school activities' in *British Journal of Learning Disabilities,* 32, BILD Publications.

Gilligan R., Curry P., McGrath J., Murphy D., Ni Raghallaigh M., Rogers M., Scholtz J.J. and Gilligan Quinn, A. (2010), *In the Front Line of Integration: Young people managing migration to Ireland* Dublin: Children, Youth and Community Relations Research Programme, Children's Research Centre in association with Integrating Ireland.

Ginsburg-Block, M.D., Rohrbeck, C.A., and Fantuzzo, J.W. (2006). 'A meta-analytic review of social, self-concept, and behavioral outcomes of peer-assisted learning'. *Journal of Educational Psychology*, 98 (4), 732-749.

Greene, S. and Hill, M. (2005). 'Researching children's experience: Methods and methodological issues' in S. Greene and D. Hogan (eds.), *Researching Children's Experience*, London: Sage.

Hernandez, D.J., Macartney, S. and Blanchard, V.L. (2009). *Children in Immigrant Families in Eight Affluent Countries: Their Family, National, and International Context*. Florence, Italy: UNICEF Innocenti Research Centre.

Holland, S. (1979) **'Rutland Street : The story of an educational experiment for disadvantaged children in Dublin'**, The Hague: Bernard Van Leer Foundation, and for the Department of Education, Ireland; Oxford: Pergamon

James, A. and Prout, A. (1997) *Constructing and Reconstructing Childhood*, London: Falmer Press.

Johnson, D.W. and Johnson, R.T. (1981). 'Effects of cooperative and individualistic learning experience on interethnic interaction'. *Journal of Educational Psychology*, 73, 444-449.

Johnson, D.W. and Johnson, R.T. (1983). *Learning Together and Alone*. New Jersey: Prentice Hall.

Johnson, D.W. and Johnson, R.T. (1985). 'Classroom conflict: Controversy versus debate in learning groups'. *American Educational Research Journal*, 22, 237-256.

Johnson, D.W., and Johnson, R.T. (1989). *Cooperation and Competition: Theory and Research*. Edina, MN: Interaction.

Johnson, D.W., Johnson, R.T., Tiffany, M. and Zaidman, B. (1983). 'Are low achievers disliked in a cooperative situation? A test of rival theories in a mixed ethnic situation'. *Contemporary Educational Psychology*, 8, 189-200.

Kagan, S. (1985). *Cooperative Learning Resources for Teachers*. Riverside, CA: University of California at Riverside.

Katz, P.A., Sohn, M., and Zalk, S.R. (1975). 'Perceptual concomitant of racial attitudes in urban grade-school children'. *Developmental Psychology*, 11, 135-144.

References

Kasinitz, P, Mollenkopf, J., Waters, M., Holdaway, J. (2008) *Inheriting the City: The Children of Immigrants Come of Age.* Cambridge, MA: Harvard University Press.

Levy, S.R., Troise, D.M., Moyer, A., Aboud, F.E. and Bigler, R.E. (2003). 'A meta-analytic review of the effectiveness of anti-bias interventions and subsequent social-cognitive developmental approach to improving racial attitudes among children'. Symposium paper presented in S. Gaertner (Chair). *Integrating Theory, Practice, and Research: A Focus on School-based Intervention programs.* Anti-bias Education: Practice, Research, and Theory, Evanston, IL.

Levy, S.R. and Killen, M. (eds.). (2008). *Intergroup Attitudes and Relations in Childhood through Adulthood.* Oxford, England: Oxford University Press.

Lipsey, M.W. and Wilson, D.B. (2001). *Practical Meta-analysis* (Vol. 49). Thousand Oaks, CA: Sage Publications.

Luddy, M. (2007) *Prostitution and Irish society, 1800-1940* Cambridge: Cambridge University Press

Lyons, Z. and Little, D. (2009) *English Language Support in Irish Post-Primary Schools.* Dublin: Trinity College Dublin.

Mandell, N. (1988). 'The least-adult role in studying children'. *Journal of Contemporary Ethnography,* 16 (4), 433-467.

McGinnity, F., O'Connell, P.J., Quinn, E. and Williams, J. 2006. *Migrants' Experience of Racism and Discrimination in Ireland: Survey Report.* Dublin: ESRI.

McGinnity, F., Nelson, J., Lunn, P. and Quinn, E. (2009) *Discrimination in Recruitment Evidence from a Field Experiment.* Dublin: ESRI.

McGorman, E. and Sugrue, C. (2007). *Intercultural Education: Primary Challenges in Dublin 15.* Dublin: Department of Education.

McKown, C. (2005). 'Applying ecological theory to advance the science and practice of school-based prejudice reduction interventions'. *Educational Psychologist,* 40 (3), 177-189.

Meade, S. and O'Connell, M. (2008). 'Complex and Contradictory Accounts: The Social Representations of immigrants and Ethnic minorities held by Irish teenagers'. *Translocations,* 4 (1), 70-85.

Merriman, B. and Guerin, S. (2006) 'Using children's drawings as data in child-centred research' in *The Irish Journal of Psychology*, 27, 48-57.

Midthassel, U.V., Minton, S.J. and O' Moore, A.M. (2009) 'Conditions for the implementation of anti-bullying programmes in Norway and Ireland: A comparison of contexts and strategies', *Compare: A Journal of Comparative and International Education*, 39 (6), 737-750.

Minton, S.J. and O' Moore, A.M. (2008) 'The effectiveness of a nationwide intervention programme to prevent and counter school bullying in Ireland', *International Journal of Psychology and Psychological Therapy*, 8 (1), 1-12.

Molcho, M., Kelly, C., Gavin, A. and Nic Gabhainn, S. (2008). *Inequalities in Health among School-aged Children in Ireland*. Dublin: Department of Health and Children.

Molcho, M., Kelly, A. Gavin and Nic Gabhainn, S. (2008). *Inequalities in Health among School-aged Children in Ireland*. Galway: HBSC Ireland

NCCA (2005). Intercultural Education in the Primary School. Dublin: National Council for Curriculum Assessment.

Nesdale, D. (2001). 'The development of prejudice in children'. In M.A. Augoustinos and K.J. Keynolds (eds.), *Understanding Prejudice, Racism, and Social Conflict* (pp. 57-73). London: Sage.

Ni Laoire, C., Bushin, N., Carpena-Mendez, F. and White, A. (2009). *Tell Me about Yourself: Migrant Children's Experiences of Moving to and Living in Ireland*. Cork: University College Cork.

O'Connell, M. and Winston, N. (2006) 'Changing attitudes towards minorities in Ireland'. In J. Garry., Hardiman, N. and D. Payne. *Irish Social and Political Attitudes*. Liverpool: Liverpool University Press.

Olweus, D. (1997). 'Bully/victim problems in school: Facts and intervention'. *European Journal of Psychology of Education*, XII (4), 495-510.

Olweus, D. (2005). 'A useful evaluation design, and effects of the Olweus Bullying Prevention Program'. *Psychology, Crime and Law*, 11, 389-402.

O'Moore, M. and Minton, S. J. (2004) *Dealing with Bullying in Schools: A Training Manual for Teachers, Parents and Other Professionals*. London: Paul Chapman Publishing.

Oortwijn, M.B., Boekaerts, M., Vedder, P., and Fortuin, J. (2008). ,The impact of a cooperative learning experience on pupils' popularity, noncooperativeness, and interethnic bias in multiethnic elementary schools'. *Educational Psychology*, 28 (2), 211-221.

Pachter, L.M., and García Coll, C. (2009). 'Racism and child health: A review of the literature and future directions'. *Journal of Developmental and Behavioral Pediatrics*, 30, 255-263.

Paluck, E.L. (2009). **'Reducing intergroup prejudice and conflict using the media: A field experiment in Rwanda'**. *Journal of Personality and Social Psychology*, 96, 574-587.

Paluck, E. L. (2006). *The Second Year of a 'New Dawn': Year Two Evidence for the Impact of the Rwandan Reconciliation Radio Drama Musekeweya.* Amsterdam: LaBenevolencija.

Paluck, E. and Green, D.P. (2008). 'Prejudice reduction: What works? A review and assessment of research and practice', *Annual Review of Psychology*, 60, 339-367.

Paolini, S., Hewstone, M., Harwood, J., and Cairns, E. (2006). 'Intergroup contact and the promotion of intergroup harmony: The influence of intergroup emotions'. In R. Brown and D. Capozza (eds.), *Social Identities: Motivational, Emotional, Cultural Influences.* Hove, UK: Psychology Press.

Pedersen, A., Walker, I. and Wise, M. (2005). '"Talk does not cook rice": Beyond anti-racism rhetoric to strategies for social action'. *Australian Psychologist,* 40 (1), 20-30.

Pettigrew, T.F. (1998). 'Intergroup contact theory'. *Annual Review of Psychology*, 49, 65-85.

Pettigrew, T.F., and Tropp, L.R. (2006). 'A meta-analytic test of intergroup contact theory', *Journal of Personality and Social Psychology*, 90 (5), 751-783.

Pettigrew, T.F., Christ, O., Wagner, U. and Stellmacher, J. (2007). 'Direct and indirect intergroup contact effects on prejudice: A normative interpretation'. *International Journal of Intercultural Relations,* 31 (4), 411-425.

Pfeifer, J.H., Brown, C.S. and Juvonen, J. (2007) 'Teaching Tolerance in Schools: Lessons Learned Since *Brown v. Board of Education* about the Development and Reduction of Children's Prejudice'. *Social Policy Report,* Volume 21 (2).

Portes, A. and Rumbaut, R.G. (2001). *Legacies: The Story of the Immigrant Second Generation*. Berkeley, CA: University of California Press and Russell Sage Foundation.

Prunty, J. (1999) *Dublin Slums, 1800-1925: A Study in Urban Geography* Dublin: Irish Academic Press,

Puma, M.J., Jones, C.C., Rock, D. and Fernandez, R. (1993). 'Prospects: The congressionally mandated study of educational growth and opportunity'. *Interim rep.*, Bethesda, MD: Abt Assoc.

Punch, S. (2002a) 'Interviewing Strategies with Young People: the "Secret Box", Stimulus Material and Task-based Activities' in *Children and Society*, 16, 45-56.

Punch, S. (2002b) 'Research with Children: The same or different from research with adults?' in *Childhood* 9 (3), 321-341.

Quinn, E., Stanley, J., Corona, J. and O'Connell, P.J. (2008). *Handbook on Immigration and Asylum in Ireland 2007*. Dublin: Economic and Social Research Institute. Page 73.

Roland, E. and Munthe, E. (1997). 'The 1996 Norwegian Program for Preventing Bullying in Schools'. *The Irish Journal of Psychology*. 18, 2, 233-247.

Roseth, C.J., Johnson, D.W. and Johnson, R.T. (2008). 'Promoting early adolescents' achievement and peer relationships: The effects of cooperative, competitive, and individualistic goal structures'. *Psychological Bulletin*, 134 (2), 223-246.

Ryan, J.B., Reid, R. and Epstein, M.H. (2004). 'Peer-mediated intervention studies on academic achievement for students with EBD – A review'. *Remedial and Special Education*, 25 (6), 330-341.

Schofield, J.W. and Eurich-Fulcer, R. (2003). 'When and how school segregation improves intergroup relations'. In R. Brown and S. Gaertner (eds.), *Handbook of Social Psychology: Intergroup Processes* (pp. 475-494). Oxford: Blackwell.

Segall, M.H., Dasen, P.R., Berry, J.W. and Poortinga, Y.H. (1999). *Human Behavior in Global Perspective (2nd edition)*. Boston: Allyn and Bacon.

Sharan, S. and Sharan, Y. (1976). *Small Group Teaching*. Englewood Cliffs, NJ: Educational Technology Publications.

References 207

Sharan, S., Hertz-Lazarowitz, R., Bejarano, Y., Raviv, S. and Sharan, Y. (1984). *Cooperative Learning in the Classroom: Research in Desegregated Schools*. Hillsdale, NJ: Erlbaum.

Singh, B.R. (1991). 'Teaching methods for reducing prejudice and enhancing academic achievement for all children'. *Educational studies* 17 (2), 157-171.

Slavin, R.E. (1978). 'Student teams and comparison among equals: Effects on academic performance and student attitudes'. *Journal of Educational Psychology*, 70 (4), 532-538.

Slavin, R.E. (1980). 'Cooperative learning'. *Review of Educational Research* 50, 315-340.

Slavin, R.E. (1983). 'When Does Cooperative Learning Increase Student-Achievement'. *Psychological Bulletin*, 94 (3), 429-445.

Slavin, R. E. (1985). An introduction to cooperative learning research. In R. Slavin, et al. (eds.), *Learning to cooperate, cooperating to learn* (pp. 5-15). New York, NY: Plenum Publishing Corporation.

Slavin, R.E. (1995). 'Cooperative learning and intergroup relations'. In J. Banks and C.M. Banks (eds.), *Handbook of Research on Multicultural Education* (pp. 628-634). New York: Macmillan.

Slavin, R.E. and Cooper, R. (1999). 'Improving intergroup relations: Lessons learned from cooperative learning programs'. *Journal of Social Issues*, 55 (4), 647-663.

Slavin, R.E., Leavey, M. and Madden, N.A. (1984). 'Combining cooperative learning and individualized instruction: Effects on students' mathematics achievement, attitudes, and behaviours'. *Elementary School Journal*, 84, 409-422.

Slavin, R., Leavey, M. and Madden, N. (1986). *Team accelerated Instruction: Mathematics*. Watertown, MA: Charlesbridge.

Slavin, R.E. and Oickle, E. (1981). 'Effects of cooperative learning teams on student achievement and race relations: Treatment by race interactions', *Sociology of Education*, 54, 174-180.

Smyth, E., Darmody, M., McGinnity, F. and Byrne, D. (2009). *Adapting to Diversity: Irish Schools and Newcomer Students*. Dublin: Economic and Social Research Institute.

Smyth, E., McCoy, S. and Darmody, M. (2004) *Moving Up: The Experiences of First Year Students in Post-primary Education*. Dublin: The Liffey Press.

Stephen, W.G. (1978). 'School desegregation. An evaluation of predictions made in *Brown vs Board of Education'*. *Psychological Bulletin*, 85, 217-238.

Stevens, R., Madden, N., Slavin, R., and Farnish, A. (1987). 'Cooperative integrated reading and composition: Two field experiments'. *Reading Research Quarterly*, 22, 433-454.

Sumner, W.G. (1906). *Folkways*. New York: Ginn.

Tajfel, H. (ed.). (1978). *Differentiation between Social Groups: Studies in the Social Psychology of Intergroup Relations*. London: Academic Press.

Tizard, B. and Phoenix, A. (1993). *Black, White or Mixed Race?: Race and Racism in the Lives of Young People of Mixed Parentage*. London: Routledge.

Wagner, U., Tropp, L.R., Finchilescu, G., and Tredoux, C. (eds.). (2008). *Improving Intergroup Relations. Building on the Legacy of Thomas F. Pettigrew. Social Issues and interventions*. Malden: Blackwell Publishing

Williams, J., Greene, S., Doyle, E., Harris, E., Layte, R., McCoy, S., McCrory, C., Murray, A., Nixon, E., McDowd, T., O'Moore, M., Quail, A., Smyth, E., Swords, L. and Thornton, M. (2009) *Growing Up in Ireland: The Lives of Nine-Year-Olds.*, Dublin: Stationery Office, 161.

Wright, S.C., Aron, A. and McLaughlin-Volpe, T. (1997). 'The Extended Contact Effect: Knowledge of Cross-Group Friendships and Prejudice'. *Journal of Personality and Social Psychology*, 73 (1), 73-90.

Yin, R. (2008). *Case Study Research: Design and Methods*. California: Sage.

Ziegler, S. (1981). 'The effective of cooperative learning teams for increasing cross-ethnic friendship: Additional evidence'. *Human Organization* 40, 24-268.